INCITING JOY

The Magic of Ordinary People

James E. McReynolds

Minister of Joy to the World

Parson's Porch Books

Inciting Joy: The Magic of Ordinary People
ISBN: Softcover 978-1-960326-25-6
Copyright © 2023 by James E. McReynolds

Parson's Porch Books is an imprint of Parson's Porch & Company (PP&C) in Cleveland, Tennessee. PP&C is a self-funded charity which earns money by publishing books of noted authors, representing all genres. Its face and voice is **David Russell Tullock** (dtullock@parsonsporch.com).

Parson's Porch & Company *turns books into bread & milk* by sharing its profits with the poor.

www.parsonsporch.com

INCITING JOY

Dedication

To all the ordinary people in the world
who have done extraordinary things.

Don't let anyone limit your potential.
Use your magic to change the world.

Contents

Foreword

Dr. John Killinger

When I suggested to prolific author James McReynolds that he write about the magic of ordinary people, I knew that he would soon be sending me a copy of his new manuscript on that subject for review.

Jim is one of the most incredible people I know. His mind is filled with all kinds of knowledge that has been shared in his sermons, in hours of psychotherapy, newsletters, and in writing articles and books. He is always actively churning with prolific stories from his research and travels.

It would be fascinating if his mind could be hooked up to a recording machine that enabled to record an endless reel of material as Jim sleeps, to see what a treasure trove of thoughts and ideas it regularly produces.

Yet, in his exceptional ability to assimilate and to reorganize materials from endless number of sources, I am sure Jim would characterize himself as one of the ordinary person. His life and experiences are not al that uncommon.

Jim has encountered most of the pains and joys we have all encountered. I am quite sure that people who have met him, would think that he is really an ordinary in spite of his books he has written, and honors accorded. People who have listened to his sermons and read his writing.

That's what makes him so special. Throughout my lifetime, I have known several great people. I have taught in several universities and served as pastor of some great churches in various parts of the country. I have met many great people. I don't think I have ever encountered another individual who is so uniquely gifted and capable of reflecting brilliantly on so many topics as Jim is.

I am always amazed, when I read one of his manuscripts, at how star-studded it is with the most apt references and illustrations.

I am honored that he thought highly enough of my suggestion about the magic of ordinary people to seize upon the idea and to produce this incredibly helpful and readable book which he created in an astonishingly brief time.

He did not merely write about the wonder and beauty of ordinary people. He wrote a book helping his individual readers to find their personal joy by exercising their God-given talents as ordinary people.

The author took my simple idea and exploded it into a sunburst of ways we can all experience more joy in our daily existence and then share that joy with others

I believe it would be impossible to read any of Jim's books without coming away filled with enthusiasm for his brilliant writing and filled with new hope for the kind of life he envious for all of us. This book, *Inciting Joy: The Magic of Ordinary People*, is no exception.

I happily give it my blessing.

"Each of us have a sense of something beyond the ordinary. Each of us have moments when something about our lives, our family, our community, our world awakens in a sense of possibility. Each of us has glimpses of that most fundamental of all possibilities that life could be extraordinary."

--B.J. Palmer

Introduction

God is glorified in ordinary people. We look on the thankless and monotonous moments as roadblocks. Ordinary days are not an interruption. They are miracles. God places human beings in so many places. God chose where you were born before your birth. We glorify God in the simplest ways.

When my friend John Killinger suggested writing a book on the magic of being ordinary, I knew he meant not just how to go from ordinary to extraordinary, but the reverse.

When we hear the word ordinary, it brings the impression about something not only common, but unnoticed, small, or unimportant. Most people think they must get away from such an existence. The ordinary kind of life is not worthy of our thoughts.

Killinger would say we should never run away from the magic of being ordinary. We don't escape the insignificant. We miss the most significant. We lose our smallness and our greatness. There is magic in being ordinary. We are the work of the Master Creator. The correct understanding of the word is that we are wonders. We are one of billions of humans, and yet each one is unique.

Instead of sitting down and waiting for life to become extraordinary, we need to take control to start finding joy in the ordinary. Make the world a better place by serving others, the whole community, and all that we touch. My wife volunteers at the community food bank. Whatever you do, be the change. Helping others is a double win.

People have enjoyed reading about ordinary people. People like themselves. If you are looking for wizard-like magic, you will have to find another book.

Embrace your child-like wonder. Children know how to find joy in the ordinary. Be excited about the magic of the mundane. I'll write more about the value of playfulness later on.

Our days need not be filled with overcomplicated plans. A kite is a magic thing to a child. It flies. As long as we are trying new things, going to new places, and discovering the world around us, we are creating magic. My daughter will remember the magic times long after I am gone from this earth.

Find joy in the ordinary by making life a game. Life can become boring at times. We can feel like we are doing the same things. We add joy into our ordinary lives by laughing more, connecting with other people, and appreciating simple things.

The Wellspring of Joy

The magic of being ordinary is discovering our uniqueness and the joy of our commonality with the rest of the human race. We must follow our joy. If we do that, life will take us on the journey that it is meant to take each of us.

Healthy means being well in more ways than just our body. Take in account our mind and spirit. Assess your own health. How we rate our health factors significantly into we address the quality of life.

Joy is a wellspring. Joy is a fundamental way of experiencing the world. Ordinary events of our journey brings that sense of wellbeing. Joy is the starting point for a connection to something that is much more sacred than our momentary emotions.

Joy brings a deeper connection with our soul. The feeling reconnects us to our true nature and our purpose. At the core of our beings, each of us wants to be connected to the highest vibrations of delight, joy, and love. We are naturally wired that way.

We remind our souls that there are no ordinary people, that there are no mere mortals. Every person is an image bearer of the most high.

Ordinary worship is glorifying God in all things. Ordinary faithfulness renews our minds. Ordinary faithfulness is enough. Magic happens in ordinary people. Inciting joy is a sensory delight.

Our greatest accomplishments will not be extraordinary things that set us apart. Choosing to be ourselves is a courageous thing. That choice makes us what the Most High created us to be. To be ordinary.

When I recently broke a bone in my foot, I had to wear a big ugly black boot. During the healing time, I appreciated being able to walk. Ordinary movement became quite important and significant. It took time to heal.

Our culture recognizes recognizable and instant results. We enjoy watching people improve. The improvement must be measured in results that are quick, easily reproductive, and measurable.

Ordinary spiritual growth is not like that. God never requires us to be successful. Ordinary faith requires faithfulness that is unremarkable love.

That sort of love is proof that we "have tasted that the Lord is good. I Peter 2:3. We become more like Jesus. God has given us everything we need for a life of godliness.

Our age or station in life makes no difference. Our background or bank account don't add a thing to our calling. Any person who is in Christ can obey with ordinary faithfulness.

Church, prayer, the scripture and the indwelling of the Holy Spirit prepare us to live the lives God has ordained for us in obedience to God's commands.

Over time, we will look more like Jesus because we have spent time looking at him. As we fix our glaze on the Christ, faithfulness flourishes.

Feeding Our Faithfulness

God desires us to feed our faithfulness. Consider the blessed man in Psalm 1. He is compared to a tree that is planted by a river. It receives regular sustenance feeding off a continuous stream of water. The psalmist tells us the Word of God is what beings about joy and faithfulness. Psalm 1:2. The tree didn't go from sapling to fully grown overnight. Because it drunk from the water regularly, it bore fruit in every season. Spiritual growth ignites joy like that. Time and nourishment are needed. Feeding our faithfulness by delighting in the Word of God creates a maturity over time.

Feeding faithfulness is not a remarkable occurrence. It's unglamorous. Feeding our ordinary faithfulness is as simple as rising out of bed in the morning to read the Bible.

Feeding faithfulness is showing up at church to hear the Word preached. It means worship with the spiritual family. We sing together, read Scripture, pray, and enjoy fellowship at the Lord's table.

God's divine power grants all things that pertain to life and godliness. God grants promise to ordinary people. Satisfaction in life involves play. Happy people play just for the pure sake of doing it. Play activities can involve what is unique for each person. These are done for fun and not for merit.

Peter goes on to write that we supplement our faith with steadfastness, brotherly affection, virtue, knowledge, and love. Ordinary obedience demands those qualities.

These are simple, everyday practices for Christians. The joy knowing Jesus more today tan you did yesterday far outlasts any approval by the world. These benefits are eternal. Philippians 3:12-13. What a joy to journey in our ordinary circumstances in faithfulness to Christ.

We will never know the ordinary people's names. Their names are written in heaven. If Paul had not named so many saints in his letters, we would not know any of them. All their devotion and works because of their faith would be completely anonymous.

The faithfulness of ordinary people would have mattered even if no one ever knew much about them. We wonder about Junia, Phoebe, Silas, and Epaphus. Most believers throughout church history were known only by God for their faithfulness.

The kingdom of heaven belongs to people all over the world. Most lived their lives with ordinary faithfulness and anonymity. What about Thomas and his ministries to India? What of the other disciples who spread the Good News on every place known to humankind?

In a culture that values extraordinary results and achievements, ordinary followers of Christ have nothing to prove. There are no instant or measurable results. It took Adoniram Judson decades before he had one convert in Burma. Disraeli wrote, "Life is too short to be little."

The Magic of Ordinary People

The magic of ordinary people helped spread Christianity throughout the world. Love created a world suited for them. Without love, the journey of life becomes dull and dead. Ordinary people pay attention to love. It is critical to feel loved by others, as it is to show love.

Ordinary people can create an atmosphere for inciting joy. Our culture tells us that there is too much competition for every dream. Every person wants the best this life journey is there to be delivered. Nobody enjoys a life of mediocrity.

There is magic in believing we can move a mountain. Most people do not believe that they can move mountains. Not many people ever do.

Ordinary people confuse wishful thinking with spiritual magic. It is true that nobody can "wish away" a mountain. The power of belief generates the skill and energy to do anything.

After college, young people start new jobs. Each wishes that someday they will enjoy reaching the top. Most really do not believe they have what it takes. Believing that it is impossible to climb higher, that don't find the steps it takes.

Others learn how to approach problems and make decisions. They believe they can do it. They expect to make mistakes. Strong belief triggers the mind to figure out ways and means that makes others have confidence in themselves. Those who think that they can move mountains, do. Those who believe they can't, cannot.

Never underestimate your own intelligence. And do not underestimate the intelligence of others. Keep your eyes focus on the important objective. If you are married, your goal is peace, calmness, and joy.

Don't be trivial. In preaching sermons or making speeches, solving problems, counseling people, think about things that matter. They think creatively. Ordinary people simply find new ways to do anything.

There are steps one can take to strengthen creativity. Believe anything can be done. This sets the mind in motion to discover a way. When we believe, our mind finds ways to do it.

Proving Things Impossible

If we think anything is impossible, our minds work to prove why. When we believe and believe deeply, something can be done. Creative solutions appear like magic. We start thinking positively and constructively. Let your mind create a way for you. Life will become stimulating, worthwhile, and rewarding.

People who say something can't be done almost always are unsuccessful, strictly average and mediocre at best. Accept negative advice only as a challenge to prove that you can do it. My mother, who had not ventured out of Southwest Virginia or East Tennessee told me that I should not expect to travel. I ended up traveling in places no one has ever done before.

Negators are found everywhere, and they delight in sabotaging the positive progress of others. If they cannot imagine doing the impossible, they won't.

I write goals at the beginning of each year. At the end of the year, I look back on them and enjoying the magic of life goals fulfilled. I am always surprised by the joy of doing impossible things.

Ordinary people don't have to dread life. Life is full of ordinary moments. These can be magical. Our world is full of wonders. Pause. Notice. Look up to the stars. Smell the air. Listen to each musical instrument during a concert. Observe the world. Choose magical mindfulness.

Welcome the ordinary joys. Learn how extraordinary and unique we are. There has never been and never will be anybody else that is just like us. Our uniqueness is expressed where we are, in the joy of the ordinary moment.

You are special. Make time for yourself. Exercise more. Eat better. Cheer others on. That is life pressure. Ordinary people feel the reality of not measuring up to being a friend, son, husband, and dad. I Thessalonians 4:11.

A few years ago, I treasured final moments with my brother David. I wrote a book titled *Joy Comes in the Mourning: Love Is Forever*. David fulfilled his purpose in amazing ways. I want to live a life as David did. He loved God. Matthew 22:37-38.

With all there is to do, David never neglected his Lord. He was a great dad. His identity was rooted in God. David's life was never filled with pride or ego. His wisdom in decision making as he found substance in solutions. He was highly effective in his work for the kingdom of heaven during his journey on earth.

You are special. Paul writes a simple reminder to Archippus to fulfill his purpose in ministry. Colossians 4:17. Don't concern yourself with what God has called others to do. Encourage and support others. Faithfully fulfill your own special ministry.

Chapter One

Inciting Joy by Having Real Friends

Faithful friendships are difficult but not impossible. Friendships are ordinary. The biblical foundation for real friendship is in the life of Jesus. Real friends dare to witness to Jesus and his final words for encouragement of his disciples. John 15:13-15. Friendship is ordinarily viewed from the secular. For Jesus and his followers, friendship is the ultimate intimacy with God. Jesus is the source and model for friendship.

The false friend will not be around in a crisis. A real friend can be counted on. Friends burst out into laughter even went in a dark time. They slap us on the back. Friends share our most precious moments. Friends incite joy in profoundly meaningful ways.

In our chaotic world, we need people who cry out with joy. In this book, we explore how ordinary Christians experience joy in our changing world.
The need to belong is fuel for being social. People with the best well-being have substantial conversations.

All of us live in differing worlds, joy is the language by which we build bridges. It is too simple to say that people in our day have no joy. They are unable to make and keep commitments. People can't live without joy.

We shall never flourish without commitment. Joy happens to ordinary people whose dreams have been shattered. We feel uncertain about the reliability of cherished institutions to nurture our desires. We have no compass in the middle of our journey. The path is not clearly marked. Finding joy in the journey becomes difficult when the signposts are barely visible.

Abraham was called a friend of God. Abraham was known as God's friend without a scripture, a church, but he sought to Know God. God tested his faith again and again throughout his life journey.

Life as a Journey

Our metaphor of life as a journey implies that there is a place of destination. Is our use of the word journey still a fitting description of the way? Where will we be when we get to where we are headed?

Grace, love, and joy is the heart and center of our soul. I wonder why so many people never speak, teach, or write about joy. Joy is at the intersection of what has been accomplished in Christ and what is to be.

In early Christian communities, as Christ's coming seemed to be delayed indefinitely, their understanding of joy changed. There have been notable exceptions, but joy has not played a central role in the writings of Christian theologians.

Joy comes as a surprising gift. Joy may spring forth at the moment when we are at the end of our rope. Joy is present in each moment of mundane, daily, ordinary life.

Joy in the deepest sense is not the same as lightheartedness. Joy is a gift. We must recognize it that way. Joy is the surprising result when the impossible becomes possible. It becomes even more surprising to a world that is coming apart at the seams. The natural tendency is to panic.

From my earliest age, I had a desire for finding friends. I was awkward and I found that people were draining. I looked for people who understood me. From childhood to college years, my friends were people I already knew. I tried connecting with acquaintances such as new people in my classes, someone in my church or interest groups.

I was too afraid to make the first mood. I just waited for others to turn toward me. I survived more than my share of awkward interactions expecting a rejection. In college, I learned a hard lesson about waiting for other people to contact me. I was comfortable with my childhood friends who I had known all my life. College brought a sea of strange faces. I felt lonely. Everyone else made friends quickly.

Upon reflection, I realized that I often don't even think about making the first move. I learned that making friends doesn't just happen. If I were ever to have new friends in my life, I would have to take courage, even if I had to step out of my comfort zone. When my wife Laurel and I first connected, she wrote a card that said, "Courage prayed help me to contact you." She and I are both introverted, and what a blessing that has been.

Jesus' life was not taken from him. He gave me it. Jesus' words invite to examine he way refer to Jesus as our friend. It means for us to love one another just as he has loved us.

To be a Christian means to know Jesus. This friendship is intimate as he incites real joy. Friendship with Jesus, and with others through his living within us, is the heart of Christian identity and practice. This intimacy is clearly seen in foot washing. The word used to describe Jesus' removal of his outer robe in John 13:4 is the same verb used in in John 10 about giving his life. (Gail O'Day, "I Have Called You Friends" in Baylor University's booklet on friendship, pp. 20-26)

23

In the gift of his life in friendship, Jesus' showed that true love is love with no limits. His friendship is more than the model for human love and real friendship. Jesus gave everything to his friends. The son gave his knowledge of God. We have been transformed by all Jesus shared with us.

Jesus' ministry was anything but ordinary. Before age 30, Jesus lived an ordinary life. He was a carpenter's son in Nazareth.

It is difficult to become a whole person unless we have friends with whom we can be ourselves. Our deepest needs are to be known and loved, to care for and be cared for. Having real friends means to know others deeply and intimately. It means to let people get to know us in the same way.

Do you belong to a group where you can hang your hat and say, "This is my place, and these are my people." They know you warts and all, inside and out. They know the dark sides of your personality as well as those dark times that you survived. Friends are there when life is stressful. Our friends help us continue to be optimistic. Positive satisfaction with life keeps us healthy. Our usual perception of changes. Friends help us see mountains, not molehills.

Life Is a Symphony

Life is not a solo, but a symphony. God never intended that we live the Christian life by ourselves. Eternal life joy is a duet, a trio, a quartet, a quintet, a choir. We are not to live like hermits. God intends for us to live together, helping each other along the way. We live together as sisters and brothers, so that we can love each other, encourage each other, admonish each other, hug each other, pick each other up, rejoice together, correct each other when we make mistakes, and weep together in the dark nights of our souls.

Our lives are not like the movies. Life has boring parts that movies do not. Ordinary moments such as a walk, a laugh, music to which we sing along. We treasure little moments. Movies are not real. They differ from the book that they are based on.

Inciting joy in today's culture is not easy. We hunger for close relationships. Yet we keep relating in a superficial way. Yearning for closeness exceeds its existence. We are not committed to long term relationships. We watch the body postures and facial movements of ordinary people. We listen to their words which indicate their inner thoughts. Some of their words do not match the experiences they describe. They are not in touch with what is going on.

We live in a lonely world. People search in bars like that one in "Cheers," the old television show. Our homes become like medieval castles. We let down the proverbial drawbridge. We go to work. We come home. We sit down. Turn on the television, read the newspaper, and go off to bed. We do the same thing day after day. More of us now depend on our personal computers and many now work from home. This trend will continue for a long while. We have no real friends, because you think you don't have to. As a result, divorce and family problems increase. Loneliness prevails. We become fragmented and disconnected.

Our relationships do not work. They don't support us. Most are demanding, absent, unloving, not to be bothered. God tells us to love everyone, even our enemies. Ordinary people get hurt and rejected. Knowingly or unknowingly withholding love is the core of rejection. Rejection takes many differing forms. People in congregations and workplaces will say unkind words. These words can be intentional or unintentional. Normally we focus our minds and attention to the rejection. I Peter 3:9

contains an effective reaction. We tend to reject back. We try harder to avoid being rejected by the congregation or those in authority by overly strong attempts to avoid more rejection in the future. The truth is we can never do enough. It can end in a living death. Living in the rejection cycle results in clinging to people who accept us, take personally everything others do or say, Fill our thoughts with worries, doubts, and fears. Rejection causes people to feel guilty. Life is just not worth it.

We become broken-world people. Most ordinary humans have been battered and bruised by sour relationships. Most friends are circle friends. These people are casual. We need intimate friends when life collapses around us. When life tumbles in, we not only find out what we are made of. We also discover what we believe in and care about.

We can reverse the rejection cycle with extraordinary love. We are deeply loved by God. This produces an overflow of love and acceptance toward others, regardless of how they treat us. God can cause even our hurt and rejection to work out for our good.

Ordinary friends are pleased to see us when the sun shines. Nobody, including Jesus, wants to suffer alone. Love means to open up to the possibility that someone will hurt you deeply. Life is never easy. So, we refuse to permit people to get close to us, because we fear that if they really get to know us, they won't like us. Ordinary life rejections cause us to be petrified if anyone comes to know us without the roles, the clothing, the fancy automobile keeps us at arm's length.

Spiritual growth becomes possible when we let other people get close enough to say the things we need to hear. We will realize the inexpressible comfort of feeling safe to unburden your heart and soul and to share the deepest secrets of your heart. Being afraid to ask for what one really wants. Instead, people sit around in hopes the relationship will be better. If we chronically ignore legitimate wants and needs. We become resentful about the relationship.

Relationships are difficult. If we cannot say no to things that are just tolerated, we will end up unhappy and bitter. Joy-filled relationships require compromise. Habituality having to compromise results in an unhealthy relationship.

We are not willing to enforce our boundaries. Healthy relationships depend on healthy boundaries. Boundaries are worthless if we do not enforce them.

In the classic love novels, an insecure, self-doubting woman meets an overly confident narcissistic man. The woman realizes that confident reassurances do not address her core insecurity. The relationship gulfs form, trust disappears, and the relationship dies.

Opposites attract. And then they explode. In the beginning, we feel good relating to someone who differs from you. Our introverted friend or partner makes it easier to participate in social events. What a temptation it is when we find a friend based on complementary traits. He or she, no matter how desirable, becomes a recipe for disappointment, distance, and resentment.

When we choose to get into a relationship, differences are appealing. They give us the illusion of filling our needs. In the long run, it is the things we agree on and share that define the strength and joy of any relationship.

We think that we are mature and intelligent decision-makers. We think that we always make important life choices rationally and objectively. We think that we have examined the possible relationship. Our unconscious patterns influence our actions more than we admit. We are surrounded by ordinary unhealthy relationships. We must change the type of people and relationships we spend time around. We find that in reality, we have low standards for emotional maturity. Just because a person is mature in one area of life does not mean they are mature in all areas of life.

Unreal expectations pave the road for disaster.

Dear reader, do you have friends like that in your life? They keep loving you when your face is in the mud. We need to be there for others when they feel finished for life. Real friends pick us up and enables us to get back in the race.

Friends are companions for life.

A faithful friend is a companion for life. No matter how bad things become, a real friend will never turn into an enemy. They love you until the end.

There is no problem we could not solve if we decided to face our problems with a friend. I have learned that none of us can get where you have been to where you want to be without somebody caring enough to help us get there. If we try to make the life journey all alone, we will not make it. Life is just too tough. A faithful friend can help us in our journey.

Being a real friend to another meets their need for friendship. Proverbs 18:24. There is great need in our culture for genuine friendship. We must have the grace to be such a friend. Philippians 1:3-8. A real friend is trustworthy. Their friendship is the best stress relievers. To make friendships and relationships rewarding we must reach out to others.

We must override reticence and shyness. We have to know how to be a friend to make a friend. Bonding is a key. Sharing each other's history. This sharing shows common interests. When we connect, we discover our likes and dislikes. Listen and learn. We must respect and value other people.

Be authentic. Every ordinary person has their own gifts and talents. Each person desires to be free of any pressure. To be a real friend takes obligation, commitment, and responsibility. Friends validate each other. They support each other's dreams.

One reason for our lack of true friends is that sometime friendship means being available at inconvenient times. Real friends are genuine. They are genuinely concerned for your welfare. If we are going to be a genuine friend, we must learn to make ourselves available. A friend is never too busy to talk. She will drop whatever she is doing, just to spend a little time to be invested in us.

Cherishing true friendship will not make the friend-seeking journey easier. Figuring out what is not desired friendship helps us clarify the meaning of true friends. Ordinary people are different from one another. When we seek friendship, we do not take educational backgrounds, interpersonal relationships, professional credibility as criteria. Love and compassion, soul nurturing, and commitment are more effective considerations.

We discover satisfaction with acceptance and approval from like-minded people. They cause us to feel secure and belonging when these people surround us. Small, shared interests lead us to overlook deeper divergencies. The feeling of being accepted and respected by like-minded people creates an illusion that we have found real friendship.

People with whom we always feel comfortable with may not become true friends. A true friend helps us to grow. Growth is ingrained with uncomfortableness.

Set principles about making friends. These are the foundations of friendship. Ordinary people prioritize these qualities differently. Being open-minded to encompass friendship is the beauty of friendship. Friendship implies vulnerability.

Sharing secrets is being vulnerable, and the bonding is gradually strengthened.

A Place for Love in the Desert

My wife and I shall never forget the Thanksgiving time we spent with our children and grandchildren in the vacation home of our San Diego family in Anza-Borrego Desert State Park. There are more than 600,000 acres containing rugged trails, incredible scenes, and night views of the sky like few other places.

Our tears flow as we remember being with the people we have loved. Family gathered from near and far. New Hampshire, Minnesota, Nebraska, Maryland, California. We missed a few who in later years gathered in our Elmwood, Nebraska home. The beautiful mountain home in California had a swimming pool. Chairs around a table gave us a place to huddle and hug each other. A blazing and inviting fire kept us warm as the desert became colder at night.

Food is always abundant with turkey or ham, vegetables, tart and sweet cranberry salad, coffee, tea, and abundant snacks. Gratitude is the only appropriate response. Our young family enjoys morning coffee. Early one morning most of the heartiest made a journey up to where the stars are shining, and to enjoy the morning sunrise. They had planned to drink coffee together, however nobody remembered to bring it along. We still laugh about that.

If we could see all our problems on a stage in a play, we would laugh. The more we know one another, the more we understand each other. Stop telling yourself that you want to change. Deep down, we want to stay the same. We remain afraid of rejection. Trust is not our normal way. We feel comfortable running the clock out on our life journey. Without friends, we stop living. The only cure for feeling inauthentic is to behave differently. Decide what type of person you want to become. As yourself what you can do now.

Life is all about relationships. We are in relationship with everything. We relate to objects, foods, weather, and transportation. Go to sleep peaceably. Trust the process to be for our good. We will cross bridges with joy and ease. We transcend our limitations.

"Chasing Cars," a song by Snow Patrol expresses idealized love. The lovely side of ignoring reality through love. It's about loving someone so intensely that we think we can't live without them. We are confused as we wonder if they feel the same way about you.

The lyrics are sung clearly.

"We'll do it all
Everything
On our own

"We don't need
Anything
Or anyone

"If I lay here
If I just lay here
Would you lie with me and just forget the world?

"I don't know
How to say it
How I feel

"Those three years
Are said too much
They're not enough

"If I lay here
If I just lay here
Would you lie with me and just forget the world?

"Forget what we're told
Before we get too old
Show me a garden that's bursting into life

"Let's waste time
Chasing cars
Around our heads

"I need your grace
To remind me
To find my own

"If I lay here
If I just lay here
Would you lie with me and forget the world?

"All that I am
All that I ever was
Is here in your perfect eyes, they're all I can see

"I don't know where
Confused about how as well
Just know that these things will never change for us at all

"If I lay here
If I just lay here
Would you lie with me and forget the world?"

"Chasing Cars" reminds me of my own searching during my times of young love. I remember the perfect blue eyes I know now it was a form of blindness. I view this song as a couple on their backs kissing near a body of water as they stare up at the moon and stars. The ground might represent reality.

The song is a favorite with college students being in love. They are scared to say those three words, "I love you." At that age, they are frustrated because of their normal and natural insecurity.

The fear of being misinterpreted, and spoiling what is, is just too much to risk. As another song my generation listened to says, "And then I said something stupid like I love you."

"Chasing Cars" is about enjoying the moment with a special person. We want to enjoy their presence without the need to talk. We are free to imagine joyful places with them. It is about growing up and finding things out. It's about making mistakes before you are too old. (Gary Lightbody and Snow Patrol, "Chasing Cars" single from album, "Eyes Wide Open.")

Fortunately, we can get better at anything with enough repetition. The only way to get better is to work differently. Face directly your insecurities where the deep pain lives. Facing a different approach. No pain. No gain. We must raise our standards. Our baseline of motivation will rise to be reality.

Relationships and connections are built into joy. We can feel quite peaceful by ourselves. Joy is a feeling we are compelled to share. Humor is frequently linked to joy. Finding ways to laugh at ourselves and our circumstances offer opportunities for joy that we naturally share.

Authentic friends value each other's friendship. They treat it gently. They strive to be in our corner. Whether you are right or wrong, authentic friends will comfort you.

Let go of the negative, manipulating, and toxic people in your life. Make room for real friends. Give them time and distance to decide if the friendship is real. The best friendships and relationships are crafted from a place of strength not weakness. Nobody likes needy friends. If a person feels they must manipulate, are revealing their deep insecurities.

A good friend is hard to find. True friendships take special and serious commitments to this most important venture. Relationships are incredibly complex. They are composed of years of experiences, memories, and interactions. Small selfless acts are incredible building blocks for relationships.

A supportive friend believes in your potential. Friends like that motivate you not to rest on your laurels. They push you to the finish line. They will go out on a limb for you. These friends are generous with their time. We need a friend who nudges us to be all we can be. They speak of us and our work in ways that causes us to blush.

When we succeed, they are proud, and they share it with others. Friends love the same things we love. When we are having a dark teatime of our soul, we feel we can call them. We share an unbreakable bond.

A picture is worth a thousand words. The spoken word is priceless. Acknowledge positive changes you spot in people. Tell them how proud you are of them. Friends could change someone's day and make an impact on the relationship with just one sentence.

If a friend can't help, they can connect to somebody who can. This extends our framework to new resources. A friend will direct us in new directions.

Friends are just plain fun. They give us a boost into positive moments. They energize us quickly when we are down. They always make us feel better. They have the remarkable ability to figure out what gives you motivation to keep on the journey.

A friend falls between intimate love relationships and casual relationships. There is a sense of mutual obligation and deep emotional ties. Friends know they can rely on each other during dark times. People who have friends live longer and healthier.

One of the measures of mental health is a person's ability to form friendships. Work, play, and intimacy are important measures of our mental health.

Without these, we keep trying to hold up what is falling down and crumbling. Our energy is spent trying to rebuild what is in shambles. Joy involves letting something beyond us come into our world of friends. We cannot hold it together by ourselves. We need real friends.

We need to tell friends how much they are appreciated. Bathe in each other's enthusiasm.

Joy is a gift that is an indication that God has incredible interest in us. The joy of the Lord is our strength, even when we are living in profound darkness when we feel like giving up.

Relationships, specifically human relationships based on mutuality and equality, help us not to go it alone. There is an Other who is important, in whom we are anchored with every fiber of our being. Eternal love and joy happens only in our relationship with others, and with God.

There is always the face of an ordinary person who looks at me and wants a level of friendship. That gazing, longing, penetrating face is a real person. The human face of the other brings me out of myself.

Our future begins in face-to-face encounters. Close friends are an important factor in how long we will live. Our lives are not only better, they also are filled with more years.

Nurturing our friendships will light the flames of joy.

Chapter Two

Inciting Joy for the Journey

Life is a journey, not a destination. There is no reason for us to live miserable lives. Integration of joy means to find joy in ordinary little events. Joy is an integral part of following Jesus. We need to stop and smell the roses. We need more spontaneity. There is an unexpected path to lasting happiness. Joy happens when we give it away. Joy shared is joy multiplied. Ordinary magic brings a flourishing life for everyone, everywhere.

Perhaps that is why my writing today is upbeat and optimistic. Jesus is not only the way, but he is the proof that there is joy in the journey. My optimistic wife and my daughter say simply, "We are on a journey to joy." On our journey, we look forward to life with God in the kingdom of heaven.

The goal of our journey is clear. Loving one another is our road to joy. This makes a difference each day in our travels. The end is joy. Jesus gives us big proof.

How do we find joy in the mundane? We get hung up on the things we are doing. We need no favorite spots to experience joy. We met God in the midst of monotony. I John 1:16. God lives within us as we are caring for those around us.

We choose hope by deciding to no longer stay stuck. I am free to discourage less and encourage more. It is easy to get lost and confused in an ordinary day. The foundation for joy is to focus on what God is telling us.

Hope anchored in heaven secures our faithfulness on earth. Our life is a journey. If your name is not known and if you have few followers, you will do special things. Your life matters because you were created in the image of God. Genesis 1:27.

We are never too old to change or to begin again. Change your commitment. Do what we have passion for doing. Keep your eyes on your life vision. Instead of running nowhere in every direction, walk in the direction you desire to go. Our vision is often limited. When we see what we see with our eyes, we might lose wonder and become narrow. That is when a little spark of joy is needed the most.

There is joy in the journey with all its wildness and wonder. God gives us light for knowing the way. There is hope for the hopeless. Ordinary people stranded by time and space are going into eternity with grace and love and joy. Our compassion will include hugging the hopeless, comforting the sad and grieving ones.

The Choice to Make the Journey Better

Life's journey becomes better when we decide to make it better. We have free will. Life is full of opportunities and challenges when we have the boldness and courage to grasp them. Finding beauty in seasons that have no loveliness requires being intentionally.

We can only control ourselves. Don't get entangled into a web of frustration. Some people visit the darkness of the past day after day. The puzzles of living can't be put together the way it was.

One of my fondest memories have been traveling across the country with the window down, the radio blasting out road songs. I felt the freedom and joy in the journey. Jesus brought joy to his and our life journeys. There are always unexpected detours, existential road construction, and unseen accidents as fender benders abound.

The lyrics of the song, "Ordinary Miracle," by Sarah McLachlan expresses what ordinary people experience.

"It's not that unusual
When everything is beautiful

"It's just another ordinary
Miracle

"The sky knows
When it's time to snow
"Don't need to teach a seed to grow
It's just another ordinary
Miracle

"Life is like a gift
They say
Wrapped up for you
everyday

"Open up and find a way
To give some of your own

"Isn't it remarkable
Like every time a
raindrop falls
It's just another ordinary miracle

"Birds in winter have their fling
Will always make it
home by spring
It's just another ordinary miracle

"When you wake up, please don't
throw your dreams away.
Hold them close to your heart
We are all a part of the ordinary miracle"

(Lyrics by Marvin Hamusch, Alan Bergman, and Marilyn Bergman)

Life is amazing and sometimes awful. Relax and exhale. Commitments and courage bring relief. Ordinary lives are beautiful and run deep. The harsh and discontent melts into magical harmony.

Our lives are not like life portrayed in movies. Life has boring parts. Movies edit them out. Hollywood dream life is not real. Life has started already. We need not wait. Live in the moment, not in the future.

Movies and their powerful music incite expectations of what life is all about. Life is never like a light bulb. It doesn't change instantly. Enjoy your ordinary life. Time is a misleading thing. We can't relive our past. We gain experience in our past activity. We can hope for a joyful future, but we don't even know if there will be one for us.

Finding joy in the ordinary is doing life differently. Switch one item or issue as you awaken for a new day. Embrace your childlike wonder. Change your routines. Laugh more

One of my oil paintings is an eerie picture of the dream life. Under it I wrote: The past is our lesson. The present is our gift. The future is our motivation.

To affirm the truth that Jesus brings joy is not to deny the tears of life, weeping that happens as a result of trials and hard times along the journey.

Those things that seek to destroy us become the things that God uses to save us.

Unbelief is our life enemy that holds us back from sharing the truth about the kingdom with those around us. The power that raised Jesus from the dead is alive and at work in mortal human beings.

Freedom, reconciliation, and flourishing are found in the kingdom. Churches and our culture elevate some voices and silence others.

The Power of Ordinary Magic

Ordinary magic is one of the most powerful forces on earth. There are no small acts. No act of goodness can ever really be considered small. Goodness triggers more goodness. It is a complete surprise just who is impacted by the succession of our simple acts. There are ripple effects in ordinary magic. Inciting joy is seen in my ministry, my friendships, my marriage, my parenting, and my relationships with colleagues.

My life has unleashed a title wave for joy around the world. I do not write in pride. Other people and God in Christ made everything happen for my good. I have benefited from moments beyond me. The grace and love of God is the catalyst. Yet, it is important that my choices played a role and made everything possible.

I have made some horrible mistakes during my lifetime. I have taken wrong turns. I have put my own human desires ahead of other people's needs.

Joy is an ember for wild, unpredictable, transgressive, but ordinary life. We want it to be extraordinary. Ordinary is the best we get. Ordinary life is heroic in its own way. That is in the face of immense pressure to imagine that we should be living in more exalted ways.

We are influenced by the opinions of others. Owning a large home or an expensive automobile bring admiration and respect. We try to impress people who should not matter.

Ordinary people pursue high-paying careers to impress others. Many find themselves trapped in unfulfilling jobs. They spend their whole life doing work that has no meaning. Spending energy to impress others quickly becomes a way to depress themselves.

Our needs to feel successful in the eyes of others causes people to have poor life choices such as a spouse, choice of friends, places to go which leads to internal resentment and bitterness and dissatisfaction.

The requirement of our culture is to be successful, to do more, to achieve more, to be a winner. Joy is composed of quiet moments for full nourishment. We miss the most important things. Going to bed exhausted and feeling guilty makes living into a dysfunctional runner on a hamster wheel. We must travel deeper in our journey. To find joy in the ordinary, slow down. Shift the focus from the doing and quiet the mind. Go outside. Open your eyes. Be patient. Notice things that incite the journey, such as a sunset, the magic of nature. The beauty of a flower. The grace of a butterfly. An ordinary life is a good life. Being average is not a bad thing.

Sit and wait. Inspiration is all around us. Advent or the Christmas season brings joy. As minister of joy to the world, I enjoy singing "Joy to the World" all year long. Joy is enhanced by the simple things. My wife and I have decorations that are beautiful. One of our trees has unique ornaments from the places we have been in the world. Our simplest touches personalize our home with warmth and love.

In all our giving, we give gifts to Jesus. I give out copies of one of my books to send a message of joy. Gifts reflect what we cherish. Lighting candles in the windows brings peace and calm. The candles remind us that Jesus is the Light. We go to see a live nativity scene. We read the Christmas story in Luke 2:1-21. We have advent candles for each moment in advent. The family will remember gathering and lighting candles for years to come. Sing Christmas songs. Play Christmas music. Surprise somebody. Call or visit someone you may have neglected all year. Sing carols in a care center. Visit those held in our prisons. Jesus came to bring joy to the world, and all heaven and nature sing. Comfort those who are feeling all alone in a hospice, hospital, or in their homes. Fill broken hearts with love.

Simple Keys to Joy

Opening the lock to finding joy in the ordinary starts with simple keys. Psalm 51:12. Joy in ordinary things is possible. An unexpected check in the mail. A phone call from your child. Love of your pet. Listening to the birds' songs. An unexpected sunrise. These are the sources for joy in your journey.

Love comes naturally and effortlessly. Love blossoms without second-guessing, calculation, or comparison. Love means to love another the way they are. It is loving even more after elaborate giving. There is no regret. Love has the power to stop the world for a moment. Love exists for the young, the middle aged, and the old.

During a Christmas in Bristol, Tennessee, I gave my mother a bottle of perfume called Joy. It cost $100 per ounce. I don't think she ever wore it. She was saving it for a special occasion. In a year or two, it had evaporated.

Finding joy in the ordinary is what pulls us on the path despite our circumstances. Ordinary joys help us come back to earth when our minds will not stop. We can focus on the little things happening right now. Give yourself the grace to take an afternoon off. We are more receptive to joy when we can unplug for a little while.

Seize the day before it seizes you. Ordinary moments that make up our everyday lives tend to be overlooked when the future seems boundless. Ordinary experiences contribute to joy as we realize our days are numbered. Life is short. Never waste a day. This my 70th year of sharing joy. 2023. Only yesterday it seems we were celebrating the grand year 2000.

Time. It is a mystery. Time was created by humankind. Ecclesiastes 3:11. Creation happened millions of years ago. God placed eternity into our souls. Knowing that eternity causes us to be uncomfortable in the measuring cup of time. The Romans said, *"Tempus fugit."* Time flies. Our months are named for life as it was during the old Roman Empire. We try to hold on to time. We created daylight savings time for human comfort. We wrestle with time. We were not created for time. Perhaps we needed time to record our history. God is not limited by time. We were created for eternity. We were made for another world.

In our journeys, we fail to notice the ordinary. God occasionally uses the extraordinary to get our attention. The favorite place for God has been in the ordinary. God wants to give us present-day awareness. God loves ordinary things.

44

Every moment of every day, every situation, every person we encounter is an opportunity to become extraordinary. Culture fills us with spectacular dreams. We were created for eternity, not for time. Time is the measure of life; we have to understand where we are and what we must do with time as it is.

Stop waiting for something to bring you joy. Slow down. Be positive. Look for joy in simple things. Seek first the kingdom of God. Inciting joy comes from our service, from spending time and listening to God. Delighting in the Word of God. Psalm 119:111. Do not lose track of the priorities. John 15:11. Never approach life from a pessimistic perspective. The day begins with waking up with gratitude for all God's blessings. Joy finds a smile on our faces.

Teaching Others to Find Joy

My calling is to teach others to find joy in the journey. A negative heart and bad attitude are big roadblocks. There is a silver lining in every dark cloud. Expect it in God's grace and love. Look at the negative experiences from a spiritual viewpoint. Romans 8:28. Most of the journey is the same for any Christian. It includes a transformation of our hearts that produces love, faithfulness, and a path that benefits others as well as ourselves. Don't journey aimlessly. Again, expect the unexpected.

Looking at our blessings during our dark times incites joy. Make a quick list of the triggers for joy. Being able to work from my home. Beautiful sunny days. An energizing nap. Seeing flowers blooming. Morning tea or hot chocolate. Glasses for better vision. Answered prayers. The love and support of my wife and children.

My readers will profit from reading *The Pilgrim's Progress* by John Bunyan who lived from 1628 to 1688. A copy of the text and a study guide for each section is offered by Chapel Library Books in Pensacola, Florida. He wrote this book from prison where he was locked away for expressing his liberty of conscience. He writes in an allegorical style, mentioning no names, but characters that represent the Christian journey. Bunyan's book has been read by millions. In his writing, he cites the essence of the ordinary Christian's journey. The work was published about 60 years after the King James Version. It has influenced the understanding of basic theology both then and now. Bunyan incited joy to the world by his words that were used in faithful preaching in the free churches. He was not allowed to be a pastor, but his writing shared the essence of the gospel for others who found places to preach.

I have enjoyed the photography of Harold Feinstein. He sparks curiosity. One black and white photograph was shot in the New York subway. The ordinary people are mere shadows heading to work with only a train ride to look forward to. They might be returning to the underground and their journey home. He shows life as it is in a particular time and place.

One photograph shows a crowd and a family looking toward the camera. A man has a cigarette in his mouth and his arm around a young woman who is holding a baby.

Often what we see is just the surface. Everyone is hurting in some way. Everybody needs praise. We are all ordinary people. We are all extraordinary in our own way. These are some lessons we can learn just by gazing at and wondering about the ordinary people. When we look at random ordinary people, some look confident, and some don't. False confidence hides insecurity. Some are highly critical. If you stop and talk to them, you experience compassion for others oozing out confidence. Their routine compassion is an outward sign of inner confidence. They show healthy humility. One day I was people watching in Washington. One young man had a neat coat that had a logo on it. He humbly said that he was John Wall. He told me he was a point guard on the NBA team, the Washington Wizards. He said he played for Kentucky. I knew that. I had seen his extraordinary play on television. He was confident with no sign of insecurity.

People like John Wall are admired as they live generous, authentic and genuine lives. Being extraordinary is not reserved for the famous, the powerful, or the privileged. People have touched us including a teacher who causes us to feel valuable, a relative who helped us believe in our dreams, a friend who created a circle of acceptance wide enough to include each of us.

Focus on the things that really matter. Intrinsic qualities bring satisfaction. Being kind and doing things for others is a trait no one can miss. It is truly a wonderful thing to be seen as imperfect. Time flies. Do not squander it. Accept that you live in a safe place. That gives us the courage to make others a priority.

We spend the days of our journey to find the times of joy. Do not temper your joy. It is not a matter of whether we deserve it. If that is our reaction, take time for gratitude and thanksgiving. Of course, joy ebbs and flows. Still we must welcome it.

We feel disconnected from our primary relationship. Such a separation poses a threat to our well-being. There is a delight that supersedes logic.

The mundane is magic. We are all an immense ordinary secret known only to God. We miss seeing the ordinary as extraordinary. Space around us can be welcoming. The rhythms of nearness and distance helps us see ordinary life in an extraordinary light.

Solitude is announcing the splendor of the ordinary and its treasure. Our separateness reveals what we hold in common. The more we journey in love, the more people, events and things disclose their hidden radiance and announce deeper meanings. We learn to see life as it is.

Our world needs people who bless every passing and yet precious moment of living. These special ones are epiphanic messengers from our Father. James 1:17. I love the word epiphany. We become a witness to the mystery of the presence of God and light in this world. Seeing Jesus is seeing the Father. Jesus was being an epiphany of e Most High.

Our ordinary existence ought to be a living example of intimacy with God and others. As our inner ears are in tune with God, we begin We enjoy every revelation in the ordinary and we hear the music of eternity. The message once garbled becomes clear.

We listen to the still small voice at the core of our being, and we respond. We have learned the wisdom of surrender.

God's silence is as intriguing as God's speaking. Silence is never a sign of rejection. Quiet rumination calms our concerns. We stop our attempts to master the mystery. We begin to appreciate the work of grace.

We feel blessed repeatedly. We stand firm in our commitment to recover the art of living. We find that Jesus is with us in the ups and downs of our journey. Faith in God carries us beyond whatever weighs us down.

God invites us to take the seed of what is missing. We release it into the foundation of our faithfulness. Choosing to forgive can soften a grace-resisting soul.

All of us seek to love and be loved. That is why the incitement of joy is so vital. Imagine how many opportunities we have lost in the journey of our lifetimes to imitate loving interchanges.

As we wait in reverence, we no longer worry about what might happen to us. Our past is behind us. The present is now. The future is I the loving hands of God. Mysteries are unfolding at our feet. Now we have eyes to see them.

Understanding deep intimacy results from listening to Christ. John 3:16-18. Jesus was willing to lay down his life for us. John 15:9-15. The downward pull of self-aggrandizement conflicts with the upward push of grace.

We need joy for the journey. We sense ourselves making progress spiritually. We feel better. Inciting joy produces openness to finding and keeping genuine friends. Unknown and known are the holy ones of God. Offer appreciation and praise. Serve God with joy. Season your path with the salt of love. Be a faithful witness to ordinary intimacy as a way toward our sanctification both humanly lived and divinely inspired.

The deep undercurrent of our love for God overflows into love for one another. This love is rarely spontaneous affinity. Love is other oriented. Love has gentleness and firmness, confirmation and affirmation.

Life is simply a lot better when we want our friends to be full of joy. Be grateful for what you have. Reframe your attitude. Your value doesn't come from external things. Your unique talents and worth can't be commodified or quantified. Friends don't need validation. Be inspired by their success. Enjoy your friends' moments of joy. Each person has a different purpose. Joys shared are joys multiplied.

Our spiritual journey is only possible if we give up our futile attempts to control relationships and instead of letting be and letting go. The journey can be lonely. Instant intimacy is our temptation if life loses its zest and becomes dull, uninspiring, and routine. We silence the whispers of the Holy Spirit. Our relationships must be modeled on Christ's capacity for redemptive love.

Love requires emotional and spiritual maturity.

Love requires emotional, intellectual, and spiritual maturity. Love is a contemplated vision of human beings. Our surrender is the beginning of a lifelong response to loving and serving others in Jesus' name. Spiritual maturity is a mystery. Grace builds on nature. In those valley times of insecure physical health and scarred emotionality, we feel the touch of mercy which results in faith. John 14:34. Faith struggles day by day as we love unselfishly. Growing in age with wisdom and grace means becoming less resistant to God's call.

Spiritual maturity calls for a willingness to be radically transformed. When we die with Christ, we rise with him in glory. God channels our weakness with saving nourishment. This becoming whole deepens from consolation to desolation to transformation.

Giving love is the opposite of selfishness. God loves us. When we know that love is inexhaustible, we won't need to go to others to get love. We go to others to give love. I Corinthians 13:4-8. This love comes from holding an attitude of humility. We need not find praise in others, remember others are important as we are. Philippians 2:3. Healthy congregational, work, and community relationships results from loving and getting along. Being secure in the love of God, we need no other security.

Transformation results in showing love to others in making allowance for their faults instead of judging and ignoring them. Ephesians 4:2. Our relationships collapse when we withhold love from others.

Once we walk the journey of maturity with Jesus, we start to change. We are givers and receivers of the love of Christ. Pain, suffering, and darkness walk beside us on the thin ice of self-sufficiency. Difficult times can be times of grace. Prayers of faith ascend to the ear of God in lightning speed. Psalm 61:2-5.

Dark nights of the soul bring fuel that powers our flight to new visions and resolutions. These experiences redeem us from superficiality to make us souls with depth. They clear the fog that obscures the inner glow of our life journey.

In those dark nights when we find no support, no help to reengage our lives. We become closed off, never allowing ourselves to be vulnerable.

The grace of God creates endurance to not just walk but to run the race to the finish, to keep on in our faithfulness. We gain a deeper calm, a miracle of grace that go beyond human understanding. The human spirit is resilient. We can reclaim our abilities to breathe, to think, to feel.

In the splendid ordinary we know joy in the air we breathe and the cooling water we drink. Ordinary is something that lacks distinctive or special features. See how nature ebbs and flows. Notice how the world is constantly changing. Be on the lookout for things that are so slightly different in the moment today compared with yesterday.

If life is feeling uncomfortably ordinary, pay closer attention to notice little things. Waiting around for the extraordinary will not help. Get in the driver's seat. Be the change.

In addition to make things better, become a nurturing soul who brings joy into the ordinary. Embrace the joy of caring for each other. One of the tools that psychologists use in their healing work is simply to advise, "Do something different."

Ride your bike to work instead of driving the car. Reward yourself for doing a job well. Shake things up to find joy in the ordinary. Today is the accepted time. It is our reality.

Embracing Child-like Wonder

Embrace childlike wonder. Do what children do. Get excited and become curious about the magic of the mundane. Try to get out of your head and notice what's around you. See things you never notice, such as a butterfly in your lawn. Wonder incites understanding. Wonder fills our passion for learning, curiosity, and adventure. Wonder surrenders to uncertainty.

During the years that I served as a therapist at Cedars Youth Services in Lincoln, I often used play therapy with children. I took several continuing education classes in play therapy. I continue to be amazed that using toys and art supplies brings healing. Breathing is deeper and slower. Downcast eyes begin to look up. Parents and other therapists hear giggles.

Child-like wonder is powerful. Some have not embraced it in a long time. After we experienced the global trauma of the pandemic, we lost our playfulness. Our time and energy ended in disappointment. Vacations, weddings, and graduation ceremonies were canceled and rescheduled. We lost the magic.

My experience is that the emotion associated with playfulness is joy. Life's destination is a playful path. The increased possibility of more moments of playfulness in the future comes simply because playing increases the likelihood of more playing.

Playfulness correlates with well-being, health, reduction of stress, better relationships, and human performance.

Make life a game. Find joy in the ordinary like winning a family contest of who can shuck corn the fastest. Who has the cleanest clothes can result from the task of washing. We all win. We are not just having fun. We are fun.

Life can be boring at times. Our life journey can feel like we are doing the same things day in and day out. There is no logical reason to accept that as the reality for living in these days. We find hope in setting realistic goals. We continue to be flexible. We discover alternate pathways.

With a passionate thrust of pure desire, we fall in love with God. Our personal vision quest is share in the "joy of the Lord" in God's transforming mission in our wounded world. As ministers of joy to the world, we give a warm and tender touch. We incite joy by being committed faithfully to our calling. This will invite love to be returned, the finest fruit that makes the ordinariness become extraordinary.

We cannot control our heredity. Our early life environments are determined for us. When I was born in Kingsport, Tennessee, my parents and I lived in a tiny one-room space. That was a humble beginning. We can control how hard we work, take risks, and follow the same roads on our journey that great people have done.

In the place where Michelangelo's David is housed, there is another statue of David. It was created by Andrea del Verrocchio. It is a prince-like figure. It has slender arms, a floral hat, and long curly hair.

Michelangelo Buonarroti concluded that the David's created by past artists were too weak and prince-like. He asked, "How could these weak-looking young men protect Florence from their enemies. Michelangelo's David is a strong and powerful sculpture. It continues to be a supreme accomplishment. He had spent more than 13 years studying the works of the masters, working with master sculptors. He found joy in his journey to greatness. He related that the secret to life success is to be ready for your time when it comes.

The Magic of Ordinary Days

An opportunity contains value that is far greater than the effort, time, and resources that are needed to seize it. Ann Howard Creel's novel, *The Magic of Ordinary Days*, is a powerful story of one woman's passion in a world at war.

Olivia Dunne never thought that World War II would affect her ordinary life in Denver. Olivia is a studious pastor's daughter who plans to become an archaeologist.

The plot thickens when an exhilarating flirtation reshapes her life. She finds herself in rural Colorado.

Olivia is pregnant. The father is an anonymous and absent soldier. Olivia marries a honest, shy farmer named Ray Singleton. Olivia has lost both of her parents. Ray is lonely living on his farm. Olivia and Ray are opposite personalities. Ray loved farming and he had no desire to be anywhere else. They sleep in separate bedrooms.

It is difficult to conceive of this arranged marriage which is not typical in our day. The novel progresses, the reader sees growth in Olivia and Ray as they come to know and accept one another. Their uncertainties, stresses, misunderstandings, and joys are believable.

Strangers falling in love through ordinary circumstances. Olivia is discontented. Her unhappiness with life comes out of her grandiose opinions about herself. She moans about what could have been. She believes she is prettier, smarter, sexually desirable, and smarter with much more potential than Ray does. Olivia's father somehow convinced this man to marry her to keep her from the same of being unmarried.

The couple is a strange match. Ray's life has revolved around his family. His life is ordinary and routine. They are uncomfortable in each other's presence. With a baby on the way, she must decide which path her journey will follow.

On an ordinary day, a young woman interrupted people eating. She had the whole restaurant down on their knees. They were looking for her earring that was lost somewhere between the entrance and the table where she was seated. Tears rolled down her face. Her voice betrayed distress at losing her valuable jewelry. It was not a high place. The prices for food were ordinary. The food was processed, not fancy at all.

Everybody looked and looked. Finally it was found by a customer in a seat near the television set. Her smile showed she was grateful. The searchers observed that the earring was nothing special. It was just a cheap, ordinary earring.

The woman offered an explanation. "I know it's just a cheap thing, but it belonged to a departed friend of mine. I was with her when she purchased it. It cost less than a dollar. She was dying and I spent days upon end with her. This earring matches the blue in her eyes."

No loss is insignificant. Losing small things in ordinary places incites joy for ordinary people. Heaven is a community where ordinary people exist with caring concern for each other. Tears shed can be wiped away. New possible things begin to emerge.

The young woman's common story shows the human need for affirmation and closeness are met. The event took place where ordinary strangers eating in an ordinary place.

While we have our peak moments, we spend the majority of our time on ordinary things. We can transform tedious tasks with creativity. That is our foundation for love. Get in touch with gratitude. Thanksgiving leads to thanks living. Being grateful will cultivate opportunities for joy in the ordinary.

Reader, I want to tell you not to stay discouraged. People need you. They truly need what you are doing. You will never see more than one per cent of the impact you have with other people. Think about tat when you become discouraged. My own dark days has taught me to never miss an opportunity to encourage somebody.

In your own vision quests, you will be opposed by sceptics, critics, plain old mean folks, cynics. People will gossip about you. Tell lies about you. If you begin to be known and perhaps honored, some will maliciously attack you in ways you never imagined. All of us have witnessed these things happening to others and ourselves. No one, not even Jesus, is exempt.

Add joy to ordinary days by connecting with others, including our children. Appreciate the simple things. Open your eyes and see what you have never seen before. Be altruistic and start having more fun today. I have shared the roadblocks because I want to keep you from disaster.

Please don't continue to be discouraged. Take time off. Rest when your body says to rest. Persevere when people attempt to destroy you. Keep on even when the demons in our pasts lure us back into their darkness. Don't listen to the inner critic that says we are unworthy or not enough.

We may be doing quite little in a little place. Persist in doing the little you can do. Resilient people are content and satisfied. There is pleasure just knowing that you have persisted through the good times and the bad times.

The words "press on" has solved many problems. The quintessential questions ask if you are satisfied with your life. Coping with the world and its direction is the other.

Becoming Bold in the Spirit

Be bold in the Holy Spirit. Being bold and resilient is an attractive thing.
We will discover new possibilities. While doing that, we will become unstuck.

This world needs a healing tonic, but the world resists. Keep on. You will be unstoppable in the eyes of others, even though it is fragile and finite in the beginning. Awaken the strength that is within us.

When I look back on my days, I see scores of ordinary people show joy, love, and goodness into my heart and soul. Most you will never see again.

Meaninglessness and hopelessness torment us. These find their ending as

Refuse to underestimate God.

Miracles still happen. The magic of the ordinary cause people to wonder and marvel at how it happened.

Decide to be the difference that makes the difference. Share the wisdom that lives in ordinary people as far and wide as possible. We can't be everything to everybody. We can always become something to someone. We are an inspiration to at least one person in the world.

Those moments will be how our world becomes all that God created it to be. When our last days on earth appear, we will not remember entire days.
Even if we live extremely numbers of days, we will cherish some moments.

The things we attempted to accomplish will pale in the end when compared to blessings given to us on our journey. Things that ultimately matter count.

Begin today to notice the important things one day and one decision at a time. Taste a little joy in your journey.

Chapter Three

Inciting Joy for Resilience

Most of us are ordinary. We have extraordinary possibilities and strengths. We all stumble and fall from time to time. Recently, I passed out in our home and bruised my face, legs, and broke ligaments in my left foot that caused fractures in my bones. My dear friend John Killinger told me the frightening experience could be a warning from God.

We are made to be able to get back up and carry on. Resilience is the capacity to live life to the fullest and to face adversity, challenge, change with determination. Downturns are not so overwhelming. Resilient people have emotional stamina and courage. Downturns are challenges to face head on and to overcome. We have no control of unexpected events such as accidents, natural disasters, crime, illness, the economy, and the fact of death.

Joy flows from the inside out. Something inside of us bubbles up and flows from our souls. Joy allows us to endure hardship and push through with resilience.

When we look on our life journey, we look back and perceive that at our most vulnerable points is when God enters our lives. Seeds of the divine and the capacities of ordinary people are found in weakness, not strength. When we are at our limits, resilience brings unexpected joy. Resilience is vitally important as our journey becomes darker.

Joy as the Bottomless Well

Joy stays ignited like a bottomless well of water. Even in our darkest days, God's joy is there. Resilient people know the joy of the Lord can't be taken away. We have the constant presence of the Holy Spirit. Grab the joy. Cease the whining and complaining. Hold onto the lifeline.

Resilience is called ordinary magic. It is bouncing back to real life while experiencing emotional distress. With wildfires raging in California and Australia, we need to be resilient. It is a human trait inhabited by all, but only used by some people. They reset their brain and change their views of the world so they can go on with their lives despite losing everything.

There are unbelievable heroic stories from California, Ukraine, and throughout the world. A nurse in Paradise, California was racing to flee the fires in the deadly fires of 2018. She called her husband from her burning car to let him know she was not going to make it out alive. His reply was, "Don't die. Run. If you're going to die, die fighting."

Resilience is important to our health. Resilience protects and reverses anxiety, depression, helplessness, fear, and negative emotions. It is the process of adapting well in times of adversity, tragedy, trauma, or significant stress.

Some people experience good outcomes in dangerous and stressful circumstances. Others do poorly and they react in ways that damage themselves physically, emotionally, and spiritually. Most people who are alive today find themselves in a survival environment. Humans have survived in all kinds of environments in all times in vastly different challenges.

Most of us do not need heroic levels of resilience in our journeys. We all benefit from more resilience with everyday stressors and challenges. Resilient people have an uncanny ability to be flexible when circumstances change. We can change ourselves, but we cannot change anyone else.

My calling as minister of joy to the world gives meaning and purpose in life. If one has no purpose life becomes futile. Purpose drives me forward.
It gives me perseverance to keep on despite difficulties, disappointment, failure, or rejection.

Purposeful people have a knack for being creative and inventive when stressful moments come. They adapt. They don't crumble. One of the principles I have shared when doing the work of psychotherapy is this: If insanity is trying to do the same thing over and over again without success, then sanity is the willingness to adapt flexibly.

God's Call to Us in Not to Be Grandiose

Our callings do not have to be grandiose. It simply means that we hold positive things in our lives that we are excited, passionate, and that we look forward toward with more motivation to persevere through our difficulties. When we are clear about our purpose, we will never lack motivation and strength.

To find strength to persevere, we start by exploring and clarifying our values which are things that matter most to you. The meaning of the life journey is finding one's gift.

Life becomes out of balance when we act with extreme responses. Believing in oneself, despite our limitations. They accept themselves with all the proverbial warts and all. Resilience is to nurture a positive view of yourself. Expect good things to happen. Process grief in a healthy way instead of running to escape it.

Resilience is a personal journey. No two people react to life situations in the same way. We must make the connections. Accepting that change is a hurdle for all of us. Thinking outside the box frees up creativity and allows effective brainstorming. Extraordinary people often see the world differently. They practice the art of critical thinking. They don't follow the opinions of others. They are in the forefront of invention.

Ordinary people have so much to contribute. They recognize their own worth. They live authentically with courage and conviction. God has given us the capacity for resilience.

The Joy of Watching Ordinary People

I enjoy watching ordinary people. Every person I meet has the possibility of a sense of awe. Everyone has overcome something which made them what they are today. We might not change the world, but for that one person you connect with, their world might be changed forever.

Every person facing adversity has used it to create meaning. They may change the way they conduct their lives. Strangers can covey comfort and give encouragement and hope to others in a ripple effect.

Resilience does not mean naïve optimism. We need not be overly optimistic or pessimistic. Accept life challenges are they really are. We will discover that we are more effective in navigated challenges.

What brought joy when you were a child? Re-imagine those earliest sparks of joy. Try out a current version of that joy. Schedule time to go try your childhood-inspired joyful activity.

Pick one totally unexpected thing to do. Just do it.

Inciting joy and success depend on the ability to see reality for what it is. My real friends have me check my interpretation of things. If I do this faithfully, my thoughts line up more closely to reality. Make a point to notice the things that bring joy.

Inciting joy on life's journey comes as we love the ordinary and the beautiful. Imagine a red rosebud, moist with morning dew. Early morning light makes it glisten. It has perfect formation, yet it is fragile. Smell its fragrance.

Ordinary magic helps us see wondrous beauty in small things. Joy is sparked in the unnoticed growth of our children. We delight in the rising sun, our child's first step, and a friend's warm embrace. We love life's small ordinary gifts. Matthew 6:25-29. Learning to see every moment of life as a small miracle that moves us to new depths of insight.

Intentional searching reveals beauty. When trees are aflame with color, we look through our windows to enjoy the wondrous display. When trees are stripped and their leaves lie brittle, we need resilience. This means purposeful searching. Finding the beauty in moments that appear unlovely requires intentional positive approaches.

Once the leaves are gone, the trees sit bare and shiver in the wind. The color fades away giving in to barrenness.

If we leave present moments, we regress emotionally. "Regression is so widespread in our culture that most people are either in the process of regressing, are in the middle of a regression, or have recently come out of a regression." John Lee, *Growing Yourself Up: Understanding Emotional Regression,* p 6.

Regression is a roadblock to resilience. By regressing we are using present day people in issues that were in our past. If we act out our negative emotions in our world, the results will hurt you. If we bottled up anger, rage is how ordinary people react. Time becomes distorted. It seems to pass quickly or drag on forever.

Resilience draws us to a depth of perseverance. We are freed by grace. We are not attached in an ultimate way to anything or anyone who is less than God. We shake off useless worry. God's resilient people live with life's inevitable limits without complaining. They are willing to alter any course of action that detracts from the freedom meant especially for them. They accept with serenity what cannot be changed. The find the courage to change what they can, and they ask for the wisdom to know the difference.

As children, ordinary people thought they never were given a choice. Adults nearly always have options.

Resilience maintains a faith perspective. From their point of view, life is no longer a struggle for isolated pleasure, power, or a goal. Everyone and everything find its place in our time allotted to us by grace.

Updated by graced moments, they are less tempted to abandon their commitments when the journey gets rough. They accept disappointment as a normal consequence of the journey. Sorrow is no reason for any setbacks. They take the peaks of the road as much as they stride through the valleys. An ordinary monk at a Benedictine monastery said that sanctification is endurance moment by moment through trials and tribulation.

Jesus gives us food for the journey on the days when we are weary. Held in Christ's outstretched arms, our resilience finds the strength and consolation we need to continue on the way. That gift grants us another blessing in our flexibility. The opposite is a deformative rigidity. Those without resilience will continue to be fixed in their ways. To flow flexibly with the wisdom of God is a challenge God's grace enables us to meet. We are familiar with the roads we take, yet we remain open to surprises. We ask God for direction. We resist the temptation to take easy detours.

It becomes less likely that the jousts of life will dampen renewed resolve. Rigid rules paralyze in a culture guided not by the gentleness of Christ, but by a functional pragmatism. Psalm 81:1-13.

Rigidity disconnects us from the whispered voice of the Spirit. That kind of willfulness blocks the ability to listen to the directives God is giving in every moment.

We can celebrate ordinary everydayness. Reality is the stuff for our spirituality. Life as it is with its many imperfections is a place for grace. Intimacy and loyalty to Christ invites us to listen, rather than growing indifferent.

God has a special purpose for our lives.

Resilience grows in the conviction that God has a special purpose for our lives. God cares for us, watches over us, and provides for us. We sense a oneness with Christ. We are open to the challenge to change. We learn to flow with grace. We celebrate everyday work and play, dancing in time to the music of eternity.

We may smile, laugh, or enjoy a short-term burst. Open your eyes to the world around us. Become attuned to the normal of life. Take off the rose-colored glasses and spot the joys. Show appreciation for others and return the kindness that you have received. Make a list of things you are grateful for. Do some random act of kindness. We can impact anyone's day. Be resilient. Don't give up. Stay strong and keep going.

Joy is subdued and we can't jump up and down. When our body is filled with unexpressed emotion, our thoughts are not clear. Ordinary people incorporate dance, movement, sound, and sight into their lives as they have been taught from generation to generation.

Some people are much more able to grow from adversity than others. All of us are well-equipped to learn from each experience. We gain personal confidence. We contribute to greater resilience in church and family, work and daily living. Every experience holds within it the potential for new growth. We are able to see beyond adversity to the reality of our common struggle as human beings.

Resilience gets us through hard times, but resilient people thrive both during and after dark times. People are not born with strong resilience. We must have unshakable beliefs. We have to maintain a positive attitude. We need to face our fears. We must not dwell or live in the past. We must remain mindful of what we take into our minds.

In the meanwhile, we live as an apprentice to love. As citizens of heaven, our hope is real and secure. Our family is so right, "There is joy in the journey."

Traces of hope remain. The signs of hope are visible in the lives of so many who live with us. Resilient people hold glimmers of hope. They shimmer with radiance as they journey onward even when everything appears lost. Some look hollow. They are lost souls. There is no sense of commitment to the future as people wander aimlessly. In Christ, there is hope. That's why I continue relentlessly to serve God as minister of joy to the world.

Resilience makes life so much more satisfying.

Chapter Four

Inciting Joy in Ministry

People who share the joy of the Lord have reasons to light the eternal flame for joy. Digging a pathway to joy is not easy. God won't force joy upon any of us. Ministry requires discipline. There is already a supply of joy. The call to ministry is a call to cultivate and practice. Joy is to be nurtured and grown.

Abiding in Christ is the best way to keep an outlook of joy. We must remain close to the Lord at all times. John 15:10-11. Seeing people come to Christ is the only reason for the existence of the church and its ministry. Mark each of these moments with joy. Luke 15:10.

Reading scripture is an incredible source of joy. Pastors and informed lay persons use commentaries, dictionaries, and many biblical resources. Just sitting back and reading the Bible is the fountain every Christian must drink from frequently. Psalm 119:162.

Singing is a way to stir up and release the joy of the Lord. When our minds are filled anxious thoughts, begin the praise God with singing. Singing allows our souls to focus on the character of God, not our circumstances. Ephesians 5:18-19.

Our joy is renewed by remembering God by meditating on specific acts of faithfulness from God. Joy never forgets to remember. Ministry is service. Jesus lived in this world not as a king, but as a servant. The heart of a servant is a joyful one.

Living each day with heaven in mind renews joy. When this world lets us down, we are reminded that God never will. Nothing is more engaging to a child as those times we put down everything and connect with them. Joy is found in those moments of spontaneity. God wants us to worship and enjoy our Supreme Being. Joy is a regular experience that no Christian, clergy or lay, can afford to miss. Only then is ministry worth it. We shall enter into joy. Matthew 25:21.

Do We Believe in Magic?

"Do you believe in magic?" was a song written in 1978 and was sung in a number of movies including *American Pie, The Parent Trap, and In America*. Ministry for most ordinary ministers had the foundation of stories of the faith found in the Bible and in Sunday School lessons. These were magical miraculous moments. Most keep looking for magic in ministry. Our preaching tends to focus on burning bushes, seas parting, and dead people resurrected to life.

I am now retired, and I am satisfied with life overall. I tried to invest in and protect my spiritual and physical health. My wife has helped me with my eating habits. Visiting physicians and dentists help in my contentment in life. Crises have come and there were times when I worked longer and harder.

Taking care of financial needs contributes to ministry satisfaction. Churches do not choose to pay their ministers a living wage. Financial limitation causes a ripple effect needing better choices. This hurts current ministries, lowers the quality of later years, and impacts future generations.

It is equally important for a minister to be content in whatever situation they find themselves in the area of finances. We knew that ministers and their families must be wise and prudent with money.

This wisdom goes on for a lifetime. Satisfaction, contentment, and comfort through the retirement years creates an atmosphere for joy.

Ministry here alludes not just to life in the church, but everything we do is a way of meeting the needs of ourselves and others. The person reading this book may clean sewers or do what has been called "dirty jobs." They do work that nobody else wants to do.

Inciting joy in ministry means being present with one another, taking care of each other in difficult and darkened days, and sharing words of peace. The magic that this world is full of is small acts of compassion shown by ordinary people. Something extraordinary happens within God's gift of grace in ordinary ministry opportunities that come each day.

Something magical happens as we fight for the rights of the poor. We are moved to help those who have lost their income. This is the kind of magic that happens in ministry. Ordinary people will find compassion, contentment, and usefulness to create a better world.

Ministry involves small acts of compassion, love, grace, forgiveness and comforting words. These can be done regardless of one's situation or circumstance.

God works through ordinary ministry.

God works through ordinary ministry. The reality is that the majority of pastors serve as workers, bus drivers, teachers, handy people, ditch diggers, anything that enables them to shepherd their congregation. There are a few churches in which hundreds and even thousands sit in the pews. However, the average attendance in the United States is less than 50. Some struggle with only one or two on an average worship day.

Intimate relationships characterize small congregations. One of my appointments in the United Methodist Church was to serve six congregations in the Blue Ridge Mountain area near Wytheville, Virginia. This pastor charge had been ever larger. They shared a minister while keeping their own buildings. They were about five miles apart. More than 55,000 Protestant churches in the United States are part of yoked or multi-point charges. That is about one-fourth of the total congregations.

My charge in Virginia were not six cloned congregations. Each had its own culture, community, setting, traditions, experiences, expectations, and style. I would preach seven or eight sermons on a Sunday. There were no identical services. Each church had its own history. Each church had its own ages, gender, experience, and worship uniqueness. Each had its own atmosphere. Some were hopeful. Some in survival mode. Some discouraged. Some like the black congregation were joyful. It was tempting to preach the same sermon. That would cut down on my preparation. Basic themes were shared in each congregation with differing atmospheres, hymns, style, and sermon illustrations. No two churches on the circuit were the same. No two faced the same issues in the same way. No sermon or ways of ministry would suit each congregation.

Ministers must guard against comparisons. They can be trouble leading to group self-importance or self-depreciation, favoritism, or complaints. Romans 12:15-16. I wrote a column for the local newspaper. Communication between each congregation must be respectful, clear, and open. Ministry in each context must be done with enthusiasm. Each church believes its pastor is deeply concerned with its needs and is committed to its well-being.

The mission of Christ is done by women and men who love out their call in their ordinary lives. The teaching and preaching of an accountant in a small church is as valued in God's sight as the wealthy evangelist or super church pastor. All have the anointing of God.

Ordinariness is projected as the opposite of specialness. Life has a definite course for each of us. It is not possible to be special as it is to be ordinary. Most people strive to be thought of as ordinary. Living up to the idea of being special is difficult. If we could be ordinary, we would not have the responsibility of living up to our potential. We can't imagine what our special role is. We declare our ordinariness when the uncertainty of the future brings anxiety and fear.

Some are more gifted than others. In the ordinary Christian church, God uses ordinary people as "priests to their God and Father." Revelation 1:5.

As ordinary churches gather, ordinary people are served in ordinary ministry. Most use ordinary means that look too simple and foolish to some. God uses them in unexpected ways. The ordinary church does not need the latest fad to draw seekers and sinners. Even an uneducated person living alone in the hills hears the story of salvation. One does not need a sensational revelation to gain assurance of salvation.

God grants mercy and grace and enlightens minds. God will honor their faithfulness and bring them home.

Think about the particular church where you are a member. If is like the majority of churches today it is not large, probably less than 40 on a given Sunday. You may be tempted to think that your church with its modest size is insignificant. Some people are embarrassed about the small size and perceived scope of the church.

When you read the word ordinary, you might mean to say typical, normal, unimpressive. The reality is that the church is the most important organization on earth. Its value and importance do not depend on size but substance. Her job is to glorify God. The church, as she is, is the bride of Christ.

If any church is preaching the gospel of good news and joy, it is not insignificant. Your small mustard seed size ministry is much more than anyone can imagine.

Dietrich Bonhoeffer's book, *Life Together*, are wise for inciting joy in any ministry setting. "A pastor should not complain about his congregation, certainly never to other people, but also not to God. A congregation has not been entrusted to him in order that he should become its accuser before men and God.

"When a person becomes alienated from a Christian community in which he has been placed and begins to raise complaints about it, he had better examine himself first to see whether the trouble is not due to his wish dream that should be shattered by God. If this is the case, let him thank God for leading him into that predicament.

"But if not, let him nevertheless guard against ever becoming an accuser of the congregation before God. Let him rather accuse himself of his unbelief. Let him pray to God for an understanding of his own failure and his particular sin and pray that he may not wrong his brethren.

"Let him on the consciousness of his own guilt, make intercession for his brethren. Let him do what he is committed to do and thank God. What may appear weak and trifling to us may be great and glorious to God." (Dietrich Bonhoeffer, *Life Together*, pp. 29-30)

Seeing David in the Stone

David Clark was the best supervisor I had at Valley Hope. David gave me a wonderful book; *Seeing David in the Stone* was written by James Swartz and Joseph Swartz. I had not read it until John Killinger suggested I attempt a book on the magic of ordinary people to bring joy to the world. The book is not written for ministers but would be the best guide to success in any job or profession. The title comes out of the work and vision of Michelangelo. He knew that there is a David in the stone. It is up to us to recognize it and make something beautiful to encourage leaders for extraordinary accomplishments. His life was lived from 1475 until 1564. The words he wrote were: In every block of marble I see a statue as plain as through it stood before me, shaped and perfect in attitude and action. I only have to hew away the rough walls that imprison the lovely apparition to reveal it to the other eyes as mine see it." (William Kondrath, *Facing Feelings in Faith Communities*, p. 185)

Every ordinary person who did extraordinary things followed the same path to greatness. Michelangelo confessed, "If anyone knew how hard and how long I have worked to become what I am today, they would no longer think such great things about me." (James and Joseph Swartz, *Seeing David in the Stone*, p. 10)

We need not be concerned about what others have been called to do. Whatever God calls us to do, faithfully fulfill the ministry given uniquely to you. Ordinary lives can produce extraordinary fruit.

This life is simply a journey. It does not matter if it is ordinary.

Chapter Five

Inciting Joy in Ordinary Congregations

Most church congregations are quite ordinary. Any change is slow and imperceptible. Whenever I visit former parishes where I have served, I sense nothing has changed. Many have died. Those that are left keep singing antique hymns. The church body keeps pushing and pushing, slower and slower. God's formula is quite simple. Stop, ask, and wait. Ask, then wait expectedly. Hebrews 11:6. God exchanges the fatigue into strength.

This book flows out of 70 years of ministry among congregations and denominations. Inspired by my friend and fellow pastor, John R. Killinger, helped incite joy and passion. I have used a spiritual strategic journey. The work was designed by George W. Bullard. I recommend reading his book, *Pursuing the Full Kingdom Potential of Your Congregation.* Ordinary congregations that are ripe to follow Christ. The program involves the most passionate members. It involves sharing a history of the church. Church members are divided into groups of three for 100 days. The group presents the congregation's future story that will shape the church's vision. Our vision became to establish an atmosphere where joy and miracles would happen.

As I grow older, I find that I am stitched into the fabric of ordinary congregations. Being a churchgoing Christian is an ordinary path. Many churches have no bulletins, piano, or basic tools for worship. Some do not have Bibles. Some have one Bible for everybody to use. The Gideons give out millions of Bibles in public and private places.

Christians in counties ruled by a dictator, where Christianity is officially banned, or live in a culture of fear and bondage dare not carry Bibles. In many places, to remain to be a Christian means to become invisible. Your name is forgotten except by the small group of people who are authentic friends.

Remaining faithful to Christ means leaving one's home, birth family, tribe, or nation. Like others have done, followers of Jesus have died in exile. There is no such thing as cheap grace, and there is no cheap friendship.

In 1948, when Chinese communists took over in insurrection, there were more than six million Christians. Not so many in the midst of more than a billion population. Christianity was a foreign religion. Missionaries and Chinese Christians were labeled imperialists. All churches were closed. Public worship went underground. People fled China and led by Chiang Kai-shek established a national government in Taiwan. There are some strong churches in Taiwan and Hong Kong. House churches continued to gather in China. Seeing that millions held on to Christin faith, China established the Three-Self movement that approved only churches listed with the communist regime.

There are many untold stories of believers as scattered seeds in exile throughout the world. One day I plan to write a book of my memoirs of international travels.

Transcending Differences

Christian fellowship transcends challenge political and social differences. Faithful friendship is not cheap or easy. Faithful friendships may not be equated with fullness of Christian fellowship. Joy was incited in me when I went on one of my family's study trips to the Russian Theological Academy in Saint Petersburg. James C. McReynolds, an Episcopalian, spent his life taking scores of ordinary people to share faith in a Russian Orthodox seminary.

Our friendship and joy were inseparable. Our vision of the family of Christ has been extended to eternity. In times of struggle, friendships testify to the grace of God and the promised kingdom. Friendship is joy in relationship with others.

Congregations do not necessarily attract the great people. It is the unknown people who have five loaves of bread and two fish who contribute to maintain the kingdom of God. John 6:5-9, Mark 6:41-44. They serve with little attention or recognition. They serve thousands. Any person who joys in the Master's touch is like the potter's clay.

With Christ's guidance, much of the menial, challenging, and hard work is done by the limited ones. God never forgets them. All gathered souls owe their growth to the devotion and faithfulness of those who have only "five loaves and two fish."

Some congregations are joyful. These are rare, but they do exist. Deep congregational joy characterizes healthy relationships. Joy is being alive to what is happening between ordinary people.

Older people are closer to God.

Today's churches are filled with people who are 50 years or older. At least they are there stuffing the pews. They have gray hair, gray suits, and gray faces. They know church is not just an amusement park. Church is a spot where different people gather to praise God. Old people are closer to God. They are not more religious.

The older folks will be seeing God face to face quite soon. Perseverance builds character. Character builds hope which never will disappoint us. Things change. God is making us into faithful people bound for glory. God never leaves us alone.

Journeying to deeper intimacy with God involves other people. People are not just an inconvenience. As we are awakened to the love of God, we become more capable of loving others and of loving ourselves. As we continue our life journey, we come to the path where God has led us from the beginning.

My wife Laurel loves to shop. I don't. I often just do people watching from a stone bench. Before my eyes ordinary people reminded me of God's love for the young and the old, the thin and the fat, the smart and the dull, the tired and the energetic, the friendly and the self-focused. Some are in wheelchairs. Some hobbling along with an ugly black boot from breaking a body part or a bone in their foot. For a few uninhibited moments, I saw God in these ordinary people.

Joyous congregations do not take themselves too seriously. They are not focused on the bottom line. They enjoy wasting time together. Vitality is a good word to describe them. Vitality means more tan survival as joy is more than breathing. A Spirit of Joy church has a meaningful existence. Sometimes the joyful congregation sets obviously unattainable goals.

These goals we set so high that ordinary means will not be achieved unless a breakthrough vision appears. During visioning quests with brainstorming and imaging settings, each member's stimulate ideas from others and new combinations are formed. Together they create images that are greater than the sum of the expertise of each individual. Creative synergy is the magic of ordinary people.

Joy is contagious. Mark Twain wrote, "To get the full value of joy. you must have someone to divide with." The Jewish celebration of Simchat Torah, held in the fall after Sukkot, is a demonstration of community joy. The name of the festival means "rejoicing in the Torah." The Torah is composed of the first five books in the Hebrew Bible. They dance together to physically and emotionally relating the Word of God to one another.

There is a dimension of joy that has deep roots connected not only to our body sensations but also faith. As people of faith, it is possible to reflect theologically on how the joy mechanism works and we are connected through our feeling to the source of joy.

Deep joy is not circumstantial. It is in relationship to our Creator, who desires for us better things than we can imagine. (Yitzhak Buxbaum, *Jewish Tales of Mystic Joy*, pp. 44-57.

Healthy congregations have a clear identity.

Healthy congregations have a clear identity. Some congregations are known for their excellence in music. Some have quality education and formation for children and youth. Some are known for outreaching into the wider community.

A mission statement and a strong vision statement clarifies one congregation from others. These incite joy for their members. It is more about being than doing. It is more like seeing a statue within a block of marble and freeing it by chipping away. A raw block of stone contains innumerable possible statues, but the faithful sculptor brings forth one statue. Any congregation has many possible identities. The responsibility to find what it believes is God's leading for its way of being and living in this particular time and place.

A faithful community brings a particular skill to their corner of the world. Communication is more direct and effective. Meetings run more smoothly. The members have a deeper relationship with one another. These congregations are more competent. They have energy and focus. They support what they create.

The congregational journey must be intentional, and the efforts need to be concerted. Clergy and lay leaders set the pace and the tone. Relationships will become stronger and deeper within the community. Decisions will be more efficient. They will know why they exist and what they have to contribute to God's mission.

After long deliberations, insights come.

Miracles happen after times of incubation. We don't always see the world as it is. Joy-filled congregations have the ability to create original images. Vision is a mental image produced by the imagination. Phil Jackson, a NBA coach who won nine world championships said, "Visions are never the sole property of one man or one woman. Before a vision can become a reality, it must be owned by every single member of the group." (Phil Jackson, *Sacred Hoops: Spiritual Lessons of a Hardwood Warrior*, p. 12)

After long deliberations, insights come suddenly when they are not searching consciously. Creative groups of people get away from their vision quest to do something that relaxes them.

Congregations can learn to envision opportunities. Lewis Carroll, a mathematics professor at the University of Oxford wrote *Alice in Wonderland*. The allegorical words were mush like those of Paul Bunyan's *Pilgrim's Progress*. Carroll wrote: "No use trying," Alice said: "one can't believe impossible things."

79

"I daresay you haven't had much practice," said the Queen. "When I was your age, I always did it for half an hour a day. Why sometimes I've believed as many as six impossible things before breakfast." (Lewis Carroll, *Alice in Wonderland through the Looking Glass*, pp. 10-11)

Warm personal relationships within the congregation are crucial if we are to work together. Positive attitudes toward one another results in constructive ways of seeking God's will together. Galatians 5:16, 22-23,25. God works powerfully as we seek divine activity among us.

To create an effective spiritual environment, we must slow down, humble ourselves, listen to one another, and seek the will of God. Prayer is vital for connecting each other to God.

The more we become one with God, we are united together. What happens to others who are living on earth with us happens to all. Seeing ourselves in others is to put ourselves in their place. New love seeps into us with awareness that God loves all of us.

Aware of this kind of love, we harbor no alienation. The world is no longer a place filled with strangers. We find community. We experience a coming together that puts us in touch with ourselves, with others, and with God.

When we are ready for a special spiritual community, it happens. We do not always have to be the ones who create a community. They appear in ordinary, unplanned, unexpected places as we encounter others.

The best untapped potentials in our churches are our infirm members. These "least" ones were spiritual giants when they had strong bodies. Old age and disease forces them to be inactive. Their spirits become as inactive as their bodies.

God still needs each one of them. What a joy to observe these bypassed people in the kingdom of heaven unfold like a red rose as they discover how much God needs them. The startling, unexpected discovery that God uses us changes our self-worth. Inherent in each human being is the need to be needed. This gives us a zest for life, and a reason for living.

These casual encounters mysteriously bloom anywhere. Hearts speak to hearts. People inevitably nourish each other in tiny congregations of one or two or in the millions who gather to enjoy a Macy's parade. Sometimes a mere touch is a spark that ignites a congregation with a sense of God.

This is a constant process within a church community. God exchanges divine presence for our loneliness. God gives he congregation power over weakness, healing for our diseases. They church body gains hope over despair, peace for anxiety, grace for our suffering, comfort for our sorrow.

Another exchange takes place when we acknowledge our inadequate ideas, our shortcomings and sinful attitudes. There is something more than what has been experienced. We find it in the mind of Christ.

Praying for others is taking others into our spot in the world. We take others into their light of God. We are drawn into a fuller love. There is no limit to the number of people who come into our circle. There are no boundaries in the love of God.

To love God is to love other people.

Inciting the joy of being loved by God makes it impossible to separate loving God from loving others. We are intimate with God. We will be surprised to find love in unlikely places.

Spiritual relationships and discernment are essential. They must be nurtured with great care.

Love is the theme of the entire Bible. There is the anticipation of some future good. Joy is tied to membership in a congregation of God's people. Individuals are part of the whole community. Both Jewish and Christian faiths affirm that we are part of a larger whole. We are to be being and building the body of Christ. It is Christ with us, inside us, and for us that makes a community.

Moments of healing and joy break into our lives. When we can't perceive the natural order of things, there are fragmentary moments of compassion and joy.

God is always walking ahead of us. God overspills our closely held plans. This is a dangerous risk. We might have to lose our familiar and comfortable images of God. The followers of Jesus demanded signs. All four gospels recount stories of the scribes and religious leaders seeking signs, proofs, or guarantees that Jesus was the Messiah.

Jesus usually refused to give signs. Tightly held expectations refuted the promises of Christ. Jesus requires entrusting of us to a way or making a way where none exists. This is what Christian commitment and faithfulness is about.

We are to participate in a life grounded in the thought that beneath and beyond all deepest longings, there is ultimate fulfillment by being united by love.

Christ's incarnation means he is much like us. He is also altogether different from us. Jesus is divine in the depths of his personality.

Our encounter with Jesus leaves a trace in us. It gives us strength about how to move toward the future. Our traces are sufficient. Christ has gone before us. Suffering and death are not the final words.

Congregations can become aware of Christ's constant coming. Romans 8:24-25. There is no magic solution as we define "magic." We incite joy by the choices we make to become the kind of congregation God desires.

A spiritual strategic journey will not be the same for every congregation. Taking time for a vision quest will result in taking the church where they could not have conceived just a few years earlier. Joy makes awareness of the presence of God.

Churches love the comfort of the present, but they are willing to be embraced by the fuzzy and unknown future. We are called to do amazing things within the fellowship of the congregation. We are called to sustain our journey, and even to perfect it.

Chapter Six

Inciting Joy in the Human Body

Inciting joy in the human body is viewed by many Christian people as incidental or inappropriate to life in the Spirit. Humans experience the world through being bodies. When we are but children, we learned to differentiate ourselves from others. We heard their voices. We touched them. If we are connected and comfortable with the body reality, we realize that we do not just have bodies. We are bodies. I Corinthians 6:19-20.

The body is a tool used for good or evil. The body was created by God. The way of unhealthy choices and it does not belong to you. Ordinary people think their body belongs to them. So they can do as they please with it.

Scripture compares our body with the metaphor of a tent. Inhabited by soul and spirit, we try to improve the body. The Holy Spirit lives inside of us. We are wonderfully made. Psalm 139:14. Our bodies are not for our own use. It is a tool to be used for God's purposes.

God created bodies to live forever. Our sin put death into the world. Bodies now decay. Our earthly tent will be taken down. II Corinthians 5:1,4. God is now making for us an eternal body. I Corinthians 15:20-22.
We must live life as God planned it. If we do, we can experience joy. Sin spoils joy. God doesn't want us to live boring lives. Enjoyment is the plan. Staying inside God's boundaries sets us free.

Joy affects the human body. There are many benefits of feeling joy. A healthier life is promoted. Joy feeling boosts our immune system. Joy fights stress and pain. And having more joy supports longevity. The power that created the human body heals the body. The magic power of all healing is love. Grace over time deepened our intimacy with our bodies. An unfit Christian needs to build up and tone down her temple of the Holy Spirit. Exercise is part of the lifestyle that keeps us well.

Joy is the feeling that comes from our potential. Joy in the human body is not a thing to be achieved. It is an experience to be lived. It is a different reality that opens us to excitement, wonder, and joy. Maya Angelou said, "We have it in us to be splendid."

Joy literally means "for the heart, in its deepest passion and feelings, to be well." Joy opens the doors for more joy. Joy is a mysterious surprise. Uncover joy. Every joy experienced is forever remembered in our bodies.

Joy shows up in the body accompanied by a smile. The corners of the mouth and cheeks rise up. Joy is associated with inner and outer warmth. We often take a deep breath when we are experiencing joy. Joy is incited by pleasant thoughts and memories, hearing a faithful friend's voice or moving music, feeling a caring touch or sensual pleasure, smelling a rose, tasting fresh fruit, seeing a loved one, a smiling child, or a beautiful landscape. Our culture and ethnicity influence the way we view the human body.

Listen to Your Body.

Listen with love to your body's messages. The body mirrors our beliefs and inner thoughts. Our body is always talking to us. Every cell in the body responds to every thought we think and every word we speak.

The body provides warning signs. When your stomach is in a huge knot or you are sweating even though today is not hot, your body speaks loudly. When our hands and feet become icy or your pulse is racing, your body is telling you that you have regressed to the point where you need attention and care. Healing. Maturing. Loving.

The joy incited with the body is feeling like we are flying, sparks and flashing lights, and ocean waves. The peak of bodily pleasure brings loss of time. We feel graced.

Older people's faces and bodies show clearly a lifetime of patterns of thinking. We need to incite joy into the human body. We make choices that benefit how we look and feel. This joy focuses on physical sensations which bring healing and transformation.

Every emotion in the body is affected by the brain. The brain does not have only one center. The frontal lobe is the control panel that monitors human emotional states. The thalamus is the information center that regulates how emotional responses are incited. There is nothing one person wants to do that the other person does not want to do.

We feel joy in the body with the release of dopamine and serotonin, the brain's transmitters. These neurotransmitters operate when simple activities such as going for a walk-in nature, petting a dog, kissing someone loved, or even a big smile help incite joy. Your face will flush, and the heart will become more intense. The face lights up. Smiling tricks the brain by elevating the mood, elevating heart rate, and reducing stress. We are lost in the eternal present. Our bodies and our nervous system are in synchrony with everything. The whole issue of mind and body dissolves.

Breathing, dilation of the pupil, digestion, and breathing happen without conscious effort. When something joyous occurs, the physical and emotional response happens right away. There is an urge to jump for joy. We may look ordinary. We are created as distinctive individuals. We have free will to choose. We can enjoy rock climbing, playing chess, reading, or writing. We feel a oneness with God. We have looked deeply inside ourselves to examine our strengths and our limitations. We are confident with sudden insights, intuition, and hunches. The process of introspection and acceptance never ends.

We are always gaining wisdom and enjoying life more as we journey on to our older years. We gain talent for absorbing all kinds of experiences. We are able to stay positive and hopeful in each time of adversity.

Joy is a state of positive effect. The body feels content, freedom, and safety. The human body finds equilibrium. Pay attention to your body. It will give us warnings, signs, and intuitive inklings about what we need to do now.

Marathon runners and joggers are not unhappy. They strain to get more air into the lungs. They enjoy exercise immensely. Their effort brings sheer joy. This is an awesome euphoric "high." This positive expectation causes some to get up before dawn day after day while others are asleep to endure pain and exhaustion.

Exercise takes the mind off worries and negative thoughts that causes depression and anxiety. Wonders are many. Nothing is as wonderful as the human body. Louise Hay wrote of the correlation between diseases and releasing the pattern in our consciousness that has created any condition in the human body. (Louise Hay, *Heal Your Body*. pp. 175-221) Her extensive list covers most everything. She loves and approves of her body. The body is a wondrous and magnificent machine.

Every cell in the body has Divine intelligence. Listen to your body. The brain is the computer of the body. Blood is joy. Veins and arteries are channels for joy. Negative thinking clods up our brain. Love and joy ordinarily flow freely and openly. Stiffness in the body represents stiffness in the soul. Fear causes us to cling to traditional and old ways. All boundaries melt away. Whenever a therapist and patient are in sync, their hearts beat in unison.

When our bodies flow while dancing, we are not listening to the music. We are acting the music. We are the music. The entire universe is dancing with us. Every second that we are alive, even if we feel we are old messes with bald heads and wrinkled faces.

Our back and spine represent our support system. Problems with the back usually means that we do not feel supported. The upper back problem indicates a lack of emotional support. Everything will be fine, because we are involved in a magical cosmic dance. We do not have to search for meaning. We become centered and content. Joy is on. Miracles and magic are pursuing us.

We find joy in a group of friends. Close relations with others bring on a life that is worthwhile. Even if people view you as unconventional, you can be independently capable. We have the possibility to lead an essentially unpredictable life. Joy keeps us moving. Joy produces bodily energy.

Bodily energy is an indication of wholesomeness. Our bodies join our minds and souls. We are well. All is well. We know that we are truly alive. Living energy is the passion that awakens our body's cells every morning flowing from our bodies and souls.

Thank the body or giving us life to do what is our purpose. The body is a temple. Give away many hugs and touches. Exercise it. Drink pure water. Restore the body with sleep.

Life is forgiving. We can reconnect with the deep inner joy we had as children. Expect an awakening or a sudden insight. We become amazed at a sunrise or sunset. Sometimes we feel the presence of somebody who isn't really there. Thoughts cease to words. They are visual images. Things that appear meaningless to others make sense. Vivid memories come with smells. The sound of a voice becomes so fascinating, I keep listening to it. Stay connected to what you love. We make deliberate choices about where we go, where we spend a weekend. Lewis Carroll incites profound awareness in our journey.

"Would you please tell me which way I ought to go from here?

That depends a good deal on where you want to go, said the cat.

I don't much care where, said Alice.

Then it doesn't matter which way you go."

We feel so vulnerable when we don't know where we should go. Growing or making a false hair is one thing we can choose. Hair represented strength to me. When we become tense and afraid, we create bands of steel in our shoulder muscles, coming over the top of the head and around our eyes. The hair shaft grows through the hair follicle. Tension in the scalp is squeezed so tightly, our hair can no longer breathe. Hair dies or falls out. New hair cannot grow. The result is baldness. Some of the princesses and princes that I have known and loved accepted their balding heads.

We are not so aware of baldness in women. Women's wigs are natural and attractive. It brings embarrassment and shame as most men's hair pieces are discernable from quite a distance. We are much too concerned about the beauty and appearance of the human body. I Peter 3:3-4.

Judging our looks based on the appearance of the ordinary people surrounding you that we see on television, in magazines, in the movies leads to wrong decisions for the body. Setting our minds on the spirit means to accept yourself and others.

Connecting Spirit and Soul with Body

We are made of spirit, soul, and body. These are interconnected. I Thessalonians 5:23. Our souls influence the human body. What we choose to think about is what we set our minds on. Scripture uses the word "fresh" as wanting our own way. I John 2:15-17. When we focus on the flesh, it brings negative consequences. This focus includes a desire to be praised and accepted by others, a drive to control not only our lives, but others as well. This focus eventually wears us out.

Feeling vulnerable or shamed curtails an inner understanding to deepen appreciation for the entire life journey. We can find a sense of safety and acceptance of who we are and the aspects of our changing bodies. The world presents impossible standards for beauty. Learning to feel comfortable and secure is important. It's vital to become less critical and more affirming. We need to let go of our unrealistic expectations for perfection. We must abandon the search for security and risk living with everything we have been given. When we observe a newborn baby transfixed by what captures her interest. We sense the unbridled joy with which a baby addresses life. We see a spark of divinity.

Never ignore the physical body

People downplay muscle strengthening and heart-pumping aerobic activity. Ordinary adults living beyond age 60 live longer than those who ignore their physical bodies.

People who have lived to age 80 and older who participate in aerobic and strengthening exercises had a much lower risk of dying from any cause. Exercise brings joy throughout the lifespan. Exercise helps human beings to flourish.

Doing excessive exercise has been proven to not be as beneficial as moderate body movement. Our exercise habits influence our sense of purpose for the life journey. We feel live has meaning, so we continue to be in motion. We continue to be active over all times. We lose our right to be a flabby Christian.

Those people who suffer from depression and anxiety tend not to work out. There are connections between exercise and negative moods. The sense of purpose is the robust experience that we get from having goals and plans to give direction and meaning to our life journeys.

Ordinary active human beings testify how exercise gives structure and meaning. Over the years, those who live active lives show more purpose and joy. Most older people report a deceasing sense of purpose. These elderly ones ordinarily have low rates of engagement in physical activity.

With more bodily joy and pleasure, they express more self-efficacy after taking up various kinds of exercise. They feel capable of setting new goals and developing a new or augmented purpose for life. I Timothy 4:8.

When our goals have a sense of deep purpose, we want to be healthy and to live long enough to fulfill them. There is nothing like the feeling you get from knowing you are in good physical condition. Waking up alert and singing in the morning, you are ready to go.

Traveling without a map

The ordinary person starts life traveling through an unmapped world with no road map. Realistically, this is the equivalent of starting off with no goals or plans. She simply figures life out as she goes along. Wishing and hoping will not make things better. Joy requires making goals.

Goals provide meaning and purpose. Goals point us to a direction. Goals energize us to feel more confident. Goals made this year increases to achieve bigger goals in the future.

Goals keep us from fearing change. We come to the assurance that life changes are self-directed. We are only happy when we are doing something that moves us toward something we desire.

Our inborn potential is extraordinary. Ordinary people have it inside them. Spend quality time to be absolutely clear about what we really want. We will unleash our potential. The body moves with the mind and soul. When our inner desire is intense, the energy and internal drive will overcome any bodily obstacles.

Getting a disease, breaking bones, hurting backs, and weak legs will not keep us from our purpose. We must move our body, or a day will come when our body won't move.

Know exactly what you want. Include improvement of health and body. Goals are defined as desired states. We must envision, commit, and plan to achieving results.

Setting goals is being alive. It brings wholeness. Achieving them feels rewarding. Gaining things like new cars, houses, and money brings no sense of well-being. On the flip side, goal setting focuses on the collective interests of other people. The most effective goals involve commitments to the will of God in our purposes, to family, to friends, and society as a whole.

If we can achieve that by setting goals, our bodies will thank us in practical and wholesome ways. Sometimes we wonder why God created us to live in our bodies, but we can't stand our physical home.

Physical body problems cause us to reject ourselves. Nobody desires to be one of those unnoticed people out there. Sometimes God makes ordinary people like you and me. God creates all kinds. Some are blessed with good looks. Some are funny looking. There are skinny ones. Short ones. Super tall ones.

As long as we think and feel like we are nothing, nowhere, nobody. God has made each of us as somebody, something, somewhere.

Chapter Seven

Inciting Joy in the Extraordinary Love Of God

God is in every way, more excellent than humans. God is not limited by time and space. God is present everywhere. We are where we are in this moment. God rules the universe. God is self-existent. No one has the power to bring God into being. Nothing keeps God living.

God incites infinite joy. The supreme artist created all things. We were created to be creative too. God creates by artistic will power. We only create with pre-existing materials. Our wisdom is limited. The wisdom of God is boundless.

Our love as human beings can be authentic and beautiful. Our love pales in comparison to the infinite love of God. We recognize that we are small. Nothing jumpstarts our sense of wonder at the extraordinary love of God like recognizing just how tiny we are in this vast universe.

Looking at the night sky at the expanse of millions of stars, we think of all the billions of people throughout the world are sharing his awesome view.

Love incites connection. Love can be cultivated. Joy is the love mood of the soul. Love builds resilience, courage, and strength. The extraordinary love from God is the ability to love for the sake of love. God never lies or breaks promises. Divine love is never moody, temperamental, or overcome by negative emotions. Our emotions vacillate. They are out of sync with reality.
Extraordinary love is not simply an emotion. It is not a body sensation. Aware and conscious it is choosing to love without

conditions. We love but not out of a special circumstance. Despite how grown up and successful we become, part of us remains a child, especially in our parent's eyes. We dads and moms never stop loving a child.

There is extraordinary love in real friendship. A friend knows the music in our heart and renders the composition back to us even when we doubt our own melody. We can do nothing by ourselves.

The covenant between a master and her or his disciple requires respect. The teachers awaken our knowledge. Humility allows wisdom to flow. The master helps us reach our highest potential.

Jesus called ordinary people to share the extraordinary love of God. During a youth retreat, young people were asked to line up from one wall in the church basement to the other wall depending on how many sexual education conversations we had with our parents concerning sexuality. Those who noted they had had "little or none" were the majority. Those who had had "lots" of conversation was filled with children of nurses and teachers. Personal comments included, "People in my church don't believe in sex." What we call "the talk" explains to youth why there is nothing healthy about casual sex. In my book on *The Silence of the Church*, I wrote, "The sound of silence is the easy way to approach the human struggle with sexuality. Churches can create an atmosphere that it is soul-healing to talk about everything else, but not about that. Many congregations are saying by this attitude that church is not a safe place to talk about our sexual selves."

The gift of extraordinary love

The minority group associated and understood sexuality as a gift of God's extraordinary love. They had shown their children how it feels to be loved unselfishly. The love of God fits in with ordinary people. Most of God's people have been simple folks. They live ordinary lives. Their lives count for eternity as they are used by God to spark joy. Scripture shows the extraordinary love of God in the ordinary. God provides everything we need for life and godliness so we can fulfill divine purpose.

God gives protection and security. Before we were born into this world, we have experienced God's protection. I have shared many stories of how God has protected me and my family. Recently, my wife and I were driving on a highway and stopped and viewed cars going both ways. When I started to move, a pick-up truck sped by and it seemed angel said, "Stop." We would have been killed without God's protection. Read Psalm 33:18-19.

With extraordinary love, God gives us daily bread. At the noon meal, Laurel and I thank God for what has been provided, for our friends and children and for a better world. The world is watching our lives. The world wants to see how the love of God has made us magically different. We will never be perfect. Those living around us watch our attitudes, our words, and our actions. Happy married couples demonstrate extraordinary love in their feelings, thoughts, and deeds in complete surrender and commitment.

Being in Love with God is joy

Being in love with God brings inherent joy. Joy is sustained in us with God's love trough the Holy Spirit. This love never wavers. The reason and basis for joy in in the love. The incarnation of Jesus is God's love brought directly to us. All human love fails. Saving and redemptive love is independent of our human desire, our efforts, and circumstances. Love incites a constant and unchanging relationship with love. God is in love with us. God will sacrifice anything for us.

Being significant to God means more than any significant friend. John 3:16. God has plans for us. Jeremiah 29:11. We are key persons to participate in something that really matters.

Love comes when we least expect it. We do not have to look for it. Hunting for love will not bring a relationship. Longing and unhappiness prevail because we do not understand that love is within us. Do not settle for anybody just to have somebody. Set your standards. Visualize what is best for you. Be ready for love when it comes. Become loving and you will be lovable. Be receptive and open to love.
If we love other people, we begin to understand what love is. Love sinks in and makes a difference in our self-images. The deepness of the love we get depends on the depth of love we give. If our love is shallow, receiving love which we receive will also be shallow.

When loves comes to you, we will know it. God never loves by accident. We shouldn't either. We choose people. We also find people God has chosen for us. Love changes lives. We must move. We have to do something.

God faithfully provides protection for our daily needs. God uses ordinary events in our lives to fulfill our purposes in the will of God. Love is the only requirement for serving God. I Corinthians 26-28.

God uses humble and ordinary people. Philippians 3:7-9. The apostle Paul used his gains, his education, his writing skills, and his speaking skills. There is a fine line between being confident in Christ and being confident in ourselves. Humility is not about denying our abilities and gifts. In grace and love, God entrusts us with talents to bring God glory.

Jesus looks for ordinary people to do extraordinary things. He overlooks flaws and weaknesses if our hearts are full of love. We must allow the Holy Spirit to shape us. Our outward behavior will reflect our inner desire. We are to empty ourselves, follow Christ's commands. Jesus is Lord. We are not.

We are to "work out our salvation" to experience saving love. We were created for love. God is love. We are God's handiwork. Ephesus 2:10. We have been appointed by God to love like Jesus does. We were created to build up people, to give love and mercy. That's extraordinary.

Gratitude is the guiding energy that makes joy possible. To know God's love, we must be aware of our blessings. That is the secret to experiencing abundant, deep, and flowing joy.

Joy will be our primary emotion in heaven. Joy is eternal because it is based on the character and nature of Jesus. John 15:11. Joy is the product of the love of God. Joy in Jesus is a secure joy because of our confidence in Jesus. John 16:16-18.

Jesus is the author and sustainer of joy. That's why joy is secured. Nothing will take it away. Joy is filled with hope in the tough times we encounter on our spiritual journey. John 16:19-22.

All of us will experience sadness and suffering. Jesus compares suffering that ends in joy to a woman in labor. The pain of giving birth is like the pain and suffering that we go through in life. These are temporary. Jesus is with us during all sorts of trials.

James 1:2. Trials produce strength. The joy of the Lord is a transforming joy in the power of prayer. John 16:23-24. This wondrous intimacy comes with the authority of Jesus. We can expect an answer. Prayer changes things. Prayer incites joy. Psalm 51:11-12. The psalmist remembered that the presence of God in prayer is the source for abundant joy. Psalm 16:11.

We will gain a sense of joy, especially when we realize that God has come through and saved us s Jesus promised. God created us out of love and joy. The Holy Spirit guides our choices day by day. Our fleeting emotions which are attached to this world will pass on with ease from our souls.

The world needs more people who have been transformed. God's love and grace sets us free from fear, insecurity, doubt, overdependence on proof and logic. Churches need leaders, by the grace of God stand at life's crossroads and choose to trust the love of God for their life.

They choose to believe that God will not abandon them. Faith trusts that God is at work in our lives. Hebrews 11:1. God is producing valuable outcomes. God's love works for good in all situations, but on the terms of God, not ours. Romans 8:28-29.

Ultimately, faithful people surrender all claims to expected outcomes in this life journey. Faith looks beyond the present to eternity, trusting that nothing will separate believers from the love of God and that God will never leave or forsake us. God works in our present circumstances for eternal purposes.

We are to keep a long-term faith perspective while we are being responsible and committed to trusting God always. Faithing is continuing to rest in the unbreakable bond of our love relationship with God.

We will keep experiencing encouragement and blessings. Jeremiah 17:7-8. Ordinary people need help to be authentic.

Our prayer is tat God will bless us with eyes to see the ways God is at work in our lives in a long-term perspective.

We must remember our limited ability to understand the will and ways of God. Isaiah 55:8-9. Beware of getting stuck on life's journey. When the events of life do not make sense, keep in mind our limitations in grasping the ways of the Lord. Proverbs 3:5-6.

Faithfulness is knowing the value of the guidance of God in little and big ways. We are not to jump to conclusions based on our understanding. Lifting our eyes off our present circumstances, we focus on God's love.

The foundation for eternal transformation

Experiencing the gospel is the only antidote to guilt and shame. The love and grace that God gives us the foundation for our eternal transformation. The more we stay on the road, the more effective we will be. Grace is about loving others as we have been loved. God loves us in our limitations, struggles, and painful times.

God affirms our complete acceptance by God's letting us know of the extraordinary love. Ephesians 3:18-19. When God speaks to us, the words affirm that we are loving children of God. Nothing we do cause God to change. We are accepted in God's eyes. I John 4:19.

Grace is about the mercy of God, our help in time of need. Our job is to seek God with all our hearts and souls. God's part is giving us the Holy Spirit and transformation. The more vital our relationship with God, the healthier our souls, the better able we are to use our gifts to become what the Creator wants us to be.

Each experience on our life journey is a fork in the road. The way we respond will make all the difference. Experiencing the immense love of God and the power of grace, we are assured of our worth in the eyes of God. Opening ourselves fully to the love and grace of God incites joy.

Since the wonderful moment of our profession of faith in Christ, the Holy Spirit has been dwelling within us. The Spirit loves us. The Spirit is an awesome gift. Romans 5:5. It is the mystery of created love.

The love of God, Jesus, and the Spirit bond us, delight us, and embrace us. That is the eternal mystery of love. We are truly blessed beyond imagination, expectation, or measure. We are blessed beyond time and space that limits us now. Eternity will forever call us, remind us, and invite us to live a life of unmatched meaning. God has placed eternity in our souls.

God in the Holy Spirit now dwells intimately with us. He loves us tenderly. The Spirit delights in us and invites us to share in eternal love. We have desires inside us which nothing in this world can bring satisfaction and contentment. We were made for another world.

Now let us look at how the work of the Holy Spirit incites joy.

Extraordinary love brings the gift of oneness

The extraordinary love brings us a sense of oneness engulfs us and we are present with unspeakable love. Extraordinary love becomes our way of being. It is a natural expression.

During worship time in the Spirit of Joy Church in my home, a college student sang her own version of "Chasing Cars," with her singing "God Chaser." This love song to God included words such as: "Lord, you are my all, everything to you I owe.

I give to you all of my life. Lord, you are my world. I don't quite know how to say how I feel. Those three words are said too much. They're not enough. Now you're mine and I'm yours. I bow my head. I need your grace to remind me that I am not alone." She sang as two of her friends played guitar and the piano. Amazing. Extraordinary. Awesome. The song reminded us that the extraordinary love of God makes all other loves have authentic meaning.

Love from God is a wonder. It incites delight. It captivates attention. Eyes twinkle. Mouths open wide. It happens when a child views her first snow fall. And she gazes at a decorated tree. Joy. Wonder.

Children of every age who see the world with wonder. They experience the surrounding environment with awe-filled surprise. To wonder is to soak up joy of any happening. Awestruck wonder is renewed wonder. Look at he wonders of the extraordinary love of God, the reason behind every good thing. Luke 2:10-14. Envision the twinkle in teary eyes, the gaping of the mouths of the shepherds.

The Creator formed us in God's image. We are fearfully and wonderfully made. Ephesians 2:10. What can we do but wonder. We embrace a child-like excitement. We are commanded gently to love God. We embrace the Supreme Being's love, and we delight in it. Joshua 22:5, Psalm 19:7-10, John 15:9-10.

Extraordinary love imparts a powerful perfume, whose smell never goes away. Its fragrance lingers as if love is not concealed once it is awakened in our heart. We use the sensory parts of our bodies. The body experiences sounds, sights, and smells. Looking at the atmosphere surrounding us from a place of wonder love makes everything vibrant. This is where the magic is.

Unconditional love will not be fully accomplished by us. God's love is our individual and community mission as human beings. We turn this essential concept into something concrete and understandable. Unconditional love looks like allowing, accepting, and embracing. Loved and loving people are safe to be around. They are safe because they are committed to expanding their capacity for unconditional and extraordinary love.

With this love in action, all wars would end. All violence would cease. This is a wonderful and courageous, and yes, vulnerable. This is the road to becoming authentic.

When we feel safe, we let down our guard. Ordinary people are messy and imperfect, but love continues to prevail. We admit our weaknesses. We own our imperfections. We feel the serenity and peace, the safety of self-acceptance and self-love.

Love comes in ordinary moments. We miss out on love and eternal joy when we get too busy chasing the eternal extraordinary. We are born to live in the body we have been given. It has to last a whole lifetime. Enjoy every day. That's the calling from God to walk daily with our Lord, talking to God, knowing and serving in this special kind of relationship. Our love needs careful and continuous tending.

Soul-mate relationships have the power to teach us about love. The journey taken in relationship removes our internal barriers to love. If we expect another to be unconditionally loving. First, love yourself, and then you can love others.

Let the Holy Spirit teach you deep expressions of love. As you grow deeper, shame is the roadblock. It is the antitheses of unconditional love. All of us have parts of ourselves that we wish were different. Doing things we wish we had done differently doesn't mean we can't know extraordinary love.

Listen to the Holy Spirit.

Chapter Eight

Inciting Joy in the Work
of the Holy Spirit

Joy is a fruit of the Holy Spirit. We cannot incite it by an act of our will. Joy comes from the Holy Spirit who works in our hearts and souls. Joy grows and prospers as we are faithful to Jesus. Jesus wanted his joy to be in us to make joy complete. John 15:11.

Scripture gives us insight into the Holy Spirit by using the dove symbol.
The dove indicates the beauty and gentleness. Matthew 3:16, 10:16. The water shows the Spirit's sufficiency. John 4:14, 7:37-38. The fire shows the Spirit's work of purification. Matthew 3:11, Hebrews 12:29. The wind indicates power. John 3:8, Acts 2:2. The seal means the security of the Spirit. Ephesians 1:13, 4:30, II Timothy 2:19. The term life means we are filled with life. Romans 8:2, II Corinthians.

The Spirit reveals God's thoughts. The work is also to help us in our weakness. Believers are filled, sanctified, sealed, and redeemed. John 14:26. Wise counsel is provided for the followers of Christ. John 16:7-8.

Some of the disciples would be recording the words of Jesus that were included in the New Testament. These were words of assurance. I own a score of Bibles with underlines and dates and places. When I have need, the Holy Spirit pulls from my memory exactly the portion of Scripture that fits my need.

In my recent years, my retiring years, I start fretting because I could remember less and less. The Holy Spirit reminded me that the spirit brings things into our memory, even in our old age. Psalm 119:11. Faithfulness includes tucking the Word of God deep in our souls by study and by memory. The Holy Spirit never makes a mistake. What we have stored in our memory blank comes clicking back to me.

The Holy Spirit causes ordinary people like me to remember not only to keep me from sinning, but to supply my needs. In adverse situations, the spirit comforts me.

The Holy Spirit frequently brings to my remembrance biblical words that I have hidden in my heart, so that I can teach others. Hiding God's Word in our hearts is important for the Holy Spirit to enable us to recall when teaching others. Jeremiah 29:11 and Romans 8:28 have encouraged me throughout my life journey.

The Spirit is God's presence in the lives of believers. I Corinthians 2:10-11. God enables to know us best through the Holy Spirit. Jesus knew that his disciples would need the power to carry out the mission to be witnesses to the world. Acts 1:8.

The Holy Spirit as Our Inner Voice

The Holy Spirit is our inner voice that whispers the truth to us about ourselves, about the things that matter to us. Whether we lead in a faith-based or a secular organization, we will be more effective as leaders when we listen to the Holy Spirit, when we value the contributions of each person involved with us. We create an environment of mutual respect.

The Holy Spirit speaks and works through ordinary people. The body of Christ is where the spirit dwells. If we neglect the Holy Spirit, the whole body suffers. Ephesians 1:17-20.

The Holy Spirit prepares us for the future. The Spirit guides believers for the good of others.

l

The Holy Spirit is at work in our ordinariness. One person lamented that we do not experience the Holy Spirit working the same miracles and divine magic today as those described in Scripture. She told me that there is something quite wrong with today's church.

The Holy Spirit directs us. He cleanses our minds. Philippians 4:8. The renewed mind opens our door to heaven. By God's grace, our souls are filled with the goodness of God. Fixing our minds on the goodness of God keeps us from wandering into paths of disobedience. Our minds are made for concentration. Concentrate on the truths of God until God blesses you. Genesis 32:26. Jacob's mind desired God. He spoke his mind which was perfectly blended with the Holy Spirit. Matthew 5:6.

Listening to others is hardest when we want to get going and produce results. We think we know the best way and we want to start now. We don't have patience with others when they don't agree with our points of view. How often have we had to slow ourselves and listen to another's Spirit-enabled input.

Listening with an open heart with a willingness to be changed by what we learn from those most directly affected. We find a much better outcome. We learn about ourselves, our methods of leading, the impact our vision have on others. We learn how non-believers experience us.

We become careful not to over-react or to react prematurely. Troubling tensions exist because of lack of understanding.

The Importance of Self-awareness

Gaining self-awareness about our strengths and weaknesses is so important. This knowledge and acceptance create an atmosphere for joy and miracles. Trust and safety, better process, and tangible results.

God wants our minds to accept divine thinking. God wants us to have minds that are clear, so that the Holy Spirit can incite words with the life of the Holy Spirit in them. Words filled with love. Joy, peace, patience, long-suffering, self-control. In other words, we speak with the mind of Jesus. When our thoughts harmonize, the joy of the Lord gives them strength. II Corinthians 5:17. Given a new mind and a new heart, we are made new. Cherish the new creature. All of heaven backs us up as our minds hold onto the words of God. Matthew 24:35, I Peter 1:25.

We agree with the Holy Spirit, and we have the Word of God to reason through the blend of the Spirit with our minds. Romans 15:5-7. If we lack wisdom, God will give it. James 1:5-8.

The mind is the seat of consciousness, of intellect, a place where the mind of God can dwell. When we are excited about something, it has our undivided attention. The mind of Christ in us helps us care for our lives, for concerns about our ways, about every word we speak, every action we take, and every expression we display. The Holy Spirit is concerned for what we are thinking. When the mind and soul are anointed, God loves to fellowship with us. That perfect blend of the human mind and the Spirit of God is a delight. To blend means to unite, to harmonize, to mix, to go well together.

If we delight in God, the Creator will give us to desires of our hearts and minds. To delight means to please. The anointing of God brings us joy for the anointing is the presence of God. Treasure and protect the anointing of God so the mind can be pure.

The eternal soul from God is the reservoir for the mind, the storage tank. There is no limit to the capacity of the soul. God keeps love and grace flowing, gushing in the soul.

Having the mind of Christ is to have a love-mind. Without it, we are spiritually crippled. When we blend our minds with the Holy Spirit and keep it blended to the anointing that delivers us. Sometimes the Spirit invades our lives in miraculous ways. Slow plodding between ordinary and the rare extraordinary is the pattern, not the exception. We live from ordinary day to ordinary day. We learn to walk by faith, not by sight. We cherish God's movements in the ordinary moments. We live in calmness and confidence.

God assures all with intimate closeness

God is always close. One day we shall see the Creator face to face. Meanwhile, we accept our ordinariness. Jesus never despises human ordinariness. From Jesus' birth until he was thirty years old, his life was quite ordinary. He chose twelve ordinary men to be his apostles.

Joy is incited as we embrace the ordinariness of life. Life will have many high points in time. Our stories will be written on tablets of human hearts with "the Spirit of the living God." II Corinthians 3:4.

Being filled with the Holy Spirit is not to be highly excited, noisy, or thinking we have sinless perfection. The Holy Spirit is powerful beyond the confines of individual Christians. My own experience of ministry taps into the mysteries of the Spirit within various communities.

The Holy Spirit works in every denomination or independent Christian place. The Spirit resides in every one of us who can cultivate the wisdom of the Spirit with simplicity and faithfulness.

The Holy Spirit often comes not in the tradition or status quo, but in social upheaval. Arenas of hostility often are in the atmosphere. The Holy Spirit inspires whole communities.

When the Holy Spirit is in action, ecstasy and restraint are present. The Spirit moves while the ordinary person lives simply. Ordinary believers have no ambition. Discouraged and energy depleted people are filled with the Spirit. The Holy Spirit comes in the power of quietness. He comes as He comes as people dance and sway in their spirit-filled worship. He comes as a small group lights candles, sings simple songs Bible reading. Their ears are alert and spirits are moved by the Holy Spirit.

Spirit-filled seekers yearn for God. We long for God. Our souls are restless until they rest in God. This longing is to become united with the magic available to ordinary people. The Holy Spirit takes us beyond our problems to creative solutions.

We discover what we are to do with our gifts and talents for the common good of human beings. Self-knowledge is the key. We acknowledge our limits while finding new potentials. The Spirit teaches us the wisdom of genuine humility. Humility is the spark that lights the fire for our ministries which are committed to loving and caring for others.

Humility and humor share the root from the Latin word humus. To be humble and to accomplish God's destiny for us is to maintain healthy humility. If we are to continue to grow in joy, we must resist self-pity. For joy to flourish, we must focus on loving God and others.

Spiritual journeys make connections in love.

Love is the foundation for connection in our spiritual journey. Love is not self-centered or shallow. Love is the link between union with God and communion with ordinary humans entrusted with our care. God gives unsparingly. Love sets us free.

God is joyful. Scripture tells us to rejoice. God shares joy as we live with the Holy Spirit inside us. Joy is not optional. Sorrow and joy are experienced at the same time. Those who have the most sorrow as they repent of their sins, feel the unspeakable joy about their forgiveness and amazing grace from God.

Without love, friendship, and family living fall apart. That's why we need ordinary people to rebuild our culture. Rebuilding is needed as only a few shares a passion for justice. Greed peels away generosity. Competition cancels collegiality.

Hopelessness does not need to prevail. We share graceful awareness as the Holy Spirit leads us through impossible challenges. Take a holy pause to reflect on where our life journey will take us. A Spirit-filled life is quite difficult, but our lives are assured to take on a new meaning.

Intimacy with God, with ordinary people, and with us cannot be rooted in human effort alone. It wells up from within us through the power of the Holy Spirit that acts in actions of grace and our response. (Adrian van Kaam, *The Mystery of Transforming Love*, pp. 44-56)

I have found an intimate connection between the work of the Holy Spirit and joy. Romans 14:17. The New Testament uniquely ties joy to the Holy Spirit. The Bible describes the Holy Spirit as a divine person distinct from the Father and Son. I Peter 1:11. Spirit of the Father in Matthew 10:20. As we write and speak about the Holy Spirit, we must realize the oneness of God.

The Holy Spirit, personified love flowing between the Father and Jesus. First John 4:16. The love of God and the joy of God are connected. This love is admiring, exciting, and delighting love. It is joyful. The Holy Spirit is the joy of God in God. Joy is at the heart of reality.

"Our responsibility is to preach and teach Christ's dynamic gospel. It is the Holy Spirit 's responsibility to make our witness effective," Bill Bright of Campus Crusade said.

When we experience the joy of the Holy Spirit, we are tasting the joy at the ultimate core. As we are transformed (or born again) we receive the incredible empowering priceless gift of the Holy Spirit who resides in us. John 3:6-7, 14:16-17. When the Holy Spirit dwells in us, both the Father and Son also live in us. John 17:20-21.

Jesus said that our experiences of the Holy Spirit would be just like "rivers of living water" within us. John 7:38-39. God's Spirit is the indwelling wellspring of joy in God as we live by faith in the son of God. Galatians 2:20. This is the joy of believing.
Romans 5:1-5.

Peter describes the ineffable joy produced by the love we experience for Jesus. I Peter 1:8-9. The New Testament is a clear record of the joy we receive from the Holy Spirit: hope in the glory of the grace of God, received by faith, which fills us with deep joy in the Spirit.

There are many human emotions. Nobody is in a joy all the time. Joy is at the heart of reality. The Holy Spirit is the ultimate joy dwelling within us. We experience indomitable joy. Spirit-empowered joy cannot be destroyed by suffering. Romans 5:3-4. Joy does not end when we are persecuted Colossians 1:24. Rejection or trials. Do not wipe joy away. I Peter 1:6-7.

"The joy of the Lord" is eternal joy. It outlasts death and increases in eternity. Romans 8:35-39. The Holy Spirit makes us new and prepared for eternal life.

The work of the Holy Spirit in a Christian's life is an ongoing process of becoming holy through sanctification.

The Holy Spirit anoints unusual people.

The Holy Spirit anoints unusual people who see a world without borders, a God without favorites, nations without boundaries. The Word of God is directed not to one nation alone, but to the nations in the whole world, all of it.

We are to preach and teach and write to unknown and inspired old women and men. Insignificant people who are waiting for a single moment when the salvation of God, which is hidden to most of the world, materializes in a single, small peasant baby who will himself be the light to all nations. (Jack Levison, *Fresh Air: The Holy Spirit for an Inspired Life,* pp. *92-93)*

As you read my books, keep a Bible with you. If you can pause for a moment, read the scripture passage that I have inserted. I am a Bible believer because the Bible has changed me by bringing to mind the words I have hidden in my heart. I am free to interpret the Bible with the presence and freedom of the Holy Spirit. We need to read, study, and devour scripture.

As a child, I used to read the Bible constantly in the family basement. I continue to read it today. I know that I must continue to be sensitive to the Holy Spirit.

God's Word is always more important than my words. Pause over ideas or my turns of phrase that attracts your attention. Think of your pauses as rest areas like those in the Great Smoky Mountains, or lookouts from a mountain road, or wherever the Holy Spirit speaks to you.

Chapter Nine

Inciting Joy in the Unexpected

We are stuck with ourselves for a lifetime, so we need to improve this relationship.

Life is a strange carousel where good and bad things come into our lives equally no matter who we are. The wheel keeps on turning. Destiny does not happen as we have expected. Life has its own rhythm. Listen. Pay attention. Look at each day with an open mind. Good things will come to us in our faithfulness and God's grace. Life is what happens to us while we are busy making other plans.

Most unexpected events are of little importance. Some are life-shaking events that cause us problems. Some are pleasant and others unpleasant. Human beings want to be in control of their lives. We feel safer in familiar environments. Surprises and unexpected events cause stress, panic, frustration, and anger.

Unexpected happenings are important in every sphere of life. What would life be without unexpected surprises? There would be no stories. Stories demand transformations, reversals of fortune, crises become challenges, and order becomes disorder. There would be little scope for sport. The results of every contest would be known in advance. New knowledge would not be created.

Unexpected surprises are not always blessings.

Surprises are not always a blessing. We don't trust the unexpected. They bring excitement, but also trouble. The best surprise is no surprise. No surprise keeps life organized and controlled. This claim means that the forces of chaos and disorder can be contained. We desire a cup of coffee or tea. We find there is no coffee nor bags of tea. We arrive at the airport and discover flights, including yours, have been cancelled or delayed.

Life is full of surprises and unexpected turns. Even if we continue to live the same type of life, dong the same routine day after day, unexpected events happen. We must accept unexpected events. They are unavoidable. Our life journeys are dynamic, not static. Our attitude is important. Some negative events are blessings. Losses and failures often leads to finding something better.

Alternate plans are necessary. First plans fail. The first plan become temporary, and it can be fixed or redone.

We can teach ourselves to accept change. Take a different route to work. Eat something different for breakfast. Go out to a concert or a movie. Take advantage of new opportunities that come your way.

Creative or differing emotional attachment helps us step back and be less affected. Build inner strength. Inner strength is most welcome in any situation. Current events lose their power and we become more composed and less agitated.

When the unexpected comes into our lives we swap the mundane and ordinary for unexpected and extraordinary. The unexpected gives benefits with enhanced joy, heightened resilience, strengthened relationships, and surprise. Surprises are unexpected and misexpected. Cognitive resources are hijacked. These are pulled into the moment.

Unexpected joy in a Missouri congregation

Theotokos Unexpected Joy Orthodox Church in Ash Grove, Missouri is a Spirit of Joy congregation. As one enters the sanctuary, there are beautiful frescos that tune into our senses with an expected delight.

Located in the Springfield area near the Ozarks, it has given unexpected joy.

"Unexpected Joy" is their vision. The prayer hanging on the wall reads," O Thou who didst make glad a great sinner with unexpected joy, and didst accept his tearful repentance, and who dost entreat unexpected mercy from Thy Son and God. Mercifully receive also my tearful signing and the sorrowful cry of my heart. Still Thou the thoughts, calm thou disturbance, and fill with quiet joy the heart that cries from the depths. Rejoice, O unexpected joy of my soul."

God uses ordinary people to do the unexpected. When ordinary people do unexpected things, it helps us believe that no matter how unremarkable I feel, God can do something extraordinary. Think of your own list of some of the unqualified and ordinary women and men that did unexpected things. Read I Corinthians 1:26-30.

Courage to keep on

They all had courage. They never let fear and intimidation silence them. They focused on God's power to calm their emotions and fears so they could think clearly.

They might have completely changed their plans. Their enthusiasm and willingness to be used by God made all the difference.

Life is full of challenges and surprises. Much of our struggle results from trying to control conditions beyond our capacity. We feel that we are in control. Unseen forces are always at work.

It is easy to use the word unexpectedly in negative ways. The stuff we own never lasts as long as we hope. In our generation, we have come to rely on more things than ever before to help us accomplish things handled more simply in earlier times.

I have purchased ten computers in my years of writing. Beyond the unexpected things lost or broken, there are so many unexpected events. Losing your job, having serious medical issues are quite common.

Accidents ruin our expensive cars, our property, and our bodies. No wonder the word "unexpected" is attached to something negative. It results in feelings of anxiety and fear. We need more control. We keep forgetting that we do not have control over much of anything except our choices and responses.

Our struggles are really pointless because nothing will change. Instead of cooperation, we fear our lack of control over our circumstances. Again, it's obvious that our journey is full of surprises that come when we least expect them.

Surprise is an amplifier. It fans positive or negative emotion. Unexpected things do not solicit emotions the same as a surprise. We choose the word "surprise" which is a bit odd.

Unexpected happenings never surprise God.

The unexpected never takes God with surprise. Trust God. The unexpected will come for all. God never promised us that the journey of life would be easy. Jesus admonished his disciples that their life would not be easy on any level. This is no less true for us, his modern-day followers.

Remember the event when Jesus was at the wedding in Cana? The host ran out of wine. When Jesus changed the water into wine, they said it was the best they had ever tasted. That magic, that miracle was not expected by those attending the wedding.

Sometimes the unexpected happens in our life journey in less dramatic ways that are no less impactful. God delights in doing the unexpected. The Supreme Being saves the best for last. God enjoys surprising us in our eleventh hours.

As we grow older, life settles. We lose our enthusiasm and passion. At all times we need to be teachable. We must be open-minded. Closed agendas, ambitions, and desire for comfort hijack our willingness. There is so much that I do not know. Ordinary people are essential to knowing the purpose of our living through the earthly journey. Everybody has a life mission.

Daily interaction with God is needed to invigorate and renew our vision quest. Step back and look at the beauty found in ordinary things. Do not let life pass you by without taking a few moments to appreciate all the wonderful things the journey of life has to offer. John Bunyan wrote an allegorical story called *Pilgrim's Progress*. As we reflect on Bunyan's writing, we notice that God gives Christian an unexpected companion named Hopeful.

Think of the times in your journey when God provided for you when it appeared that all hope was gone. The surprising aspect is that God's providential care came through ordinary people and circumstances. Hopeful told Christian that there were many in the fair that would take their time and follow as authentic friends. Christian had lost Faithful as Faithful was

118

murdered by the citizens of Vanity where there abounded temptations in their lust-filled fair.

Think back in the past when something unexpected left a mark on your life. Perhaps it was a chance meeting with a person who became your spouse. John Lennon sang, "Life is what happens to you while you are bust making other plans." Any hour, any day, any month, any year might be planned for, but unexpected things are bound to happen. We rarely expect our circumstances to develop as they do. Joy is incited as a wonderful surprise.

I have become amazed at the serendipitous surprises. Anxiety, fear, stress, contention and uncertainty disappear. Possibilities, peace, satisfaction, effectiveness and sheer joy become real. It is quite normal to have expectations, but we should never be bound by them. Something better could unfold for us. The path will bring more struggle if we expect life to develop in a particular way.

Life surprises us when we leave our comfort zone. Within the circle of ordinary people, someone will be there to limit your personal growth. We must leave many desirable things behind us, even people. The creative force that resides within us enables us to have courage, break routines, and change our thinking.

Limiting thoughts are negative ideas that are considered as facts. These condition our lives. One horrific bad experience or difficult childhood. Limiting beliefs block us from new opportunities. There are no roadmaps that reveal our future.

Real life is not defined by our failures and mistakes. Grace is walking freely, free of resentments and guilt. Igniting joy is wrapped up in our positive beliefs. The point of the life journey is believing in ourselves and creating the person God meant for us to be.

We have no control over the outcome. When things do not happen, our emotional reaction is less severe. Hope for the best. Don't expect it.

Brooding over past mistakes, failures, and missed opportunities gives us the illusion that we are in control. Brooding is unhealthy thinking abut an imagined future. Our minds become chaotic, noisy, and stressful.

To incite joy there must be space for wonder. An old rodeo bull rider and horse trainer says that living in reality is choosing to sit in the saddle in the direction the horse is going. There are surprises which each moment suddenly brings like the unexpected move of a rodeo bull. We can't hold on to unrealistic expectations of how we think living should be. Romans 8:28. Everything happens for a reason. Everybody resists life surprises,
the wonders for living for their own reasons.

Take each moment as it is. Moments unravel from our hands because we have devoted our attention to what we anticipate is looming next. The obstacles we fear may lead us to our riding a bull successfully or falling off in pain.

Untangling from expectations

Inciting joy comes when we untangle ourselves from expectations. Lean toward those discomforts of life. Our journey is made up of spontaneous changes. Let reality be natural reality. Don't try to resist it. Life is simple. Everything happens for us, not to us.

We might resist warnings during a winter snowstorm. If we resist the warnings and go on our way, that decision could be a fatal one. Warnings are signals to not resist the reality of the present moment.

Much of our pain and suffering occurs from resistance to what is. Life is.
The unexpected causes our emotions to intensify. We feel deeper joy than we ordinarily would know. If we were surprised by some unexpected negative thing, feelings of anger and despair will intensify because of the surprise. The more we expect something, the less we are surprised.

We try to get away from bad things. When we do, those moments tighten their holds on us. My chiropractor Dr. Bryan Hufstader advised me that the amount of stress in my life is determined by how much energy we spend in resistance. The more we resist life circumstances, the more stress we experience.

Life is full of surprises and unexpected turns. Our journeys are filled with frequent issues. Unexpected interruptions cause panic, frustration, anger, and they are unavoidable. Accepting this reality makes acceptance easier. Life is always dynamic, never static. The sooner we accept and acknowledge, the better we will deal with changes with a positive attitude. This attitude is our best asset in unexpected situations. Go where love is. God's love is continually available, close, and filled with grace. There is nothing we can do to earn the love of God. Nothing is more important than making space for God. Make that space any way we envision. Who knows what will happen if immerse ourselves in the love and presence of God.

We sense God in the same ways we saw God in the past. We see what we have come to expect. We are not willing to be surprised. Our vision quest requires that we pay close attention to the unexpected. To expect God no matter where we are is wearing blinders.

We must become willing to be surprised. That is just when we receive the unexpected. None of this happens overnight. We learn new behavior in the same way a child does. We grow through our openness to vulnerability. Self-revelation and vulnerability bring intimacy. Without these things, we become frozen inside.

We must turn loose our rigid control and reveal ourselves. Simply let go and trust God. When we do, it will be like a dam bursting loose. James 4:8.

Even the negative events turn to progress and success. Persistence and motivation replace helplessness, fear, and ignorance about what to do next. Look at whatever happens. Think constructively about your next step.

Focus on the present moment. To dwell fully in the moment we are in, listening in the midst of ordinary time. Make the most of how life is now. A certain amount of emotional detachment helps us from being affected. This keeps us calm and enable a foundation of inner strength. Each person is a living word, spoken by God with tenderness and love. Unexpected joy is incited as we are rooted in love. God sings love songs to us. Isaiah 5:1. Nothing is more healing than hearing the love songs from God. God places onto us a garment of love.

The sounds we hear help us become born anew. Moments when we are alone with God without anything else including time, inner compulsions, cause us to become absorbed in the present moment. We listen and delight. We are renewed by ordinary simplicity.

Love is like a butterfly.

When we expect God to act and love only as we think love should be, we might be disappointed. God is cherishing us in every moment with deep love. God loved us first. This love is found at all times and in all places. "Love is like a butterfly," Dolly Partin sings. My grandson Ethan has always loved butterflies.

When he was about five or six years old, his little nose was pressing against the glass window. Always curious and alert to life around him, he was watching a butterfly with complete absorption.

That's a wonderful illustration of being there with God. Like Ethan, we put our noses against the windows not knowing what unexpectedly brings us joy. Being present to God is being present to everything and everyone who comes unexpectantly into our lives. Isaiah 60:4.

We are connected with other people. We are drawn toward others, not away from them. We will sense a puzzling sense of love for everyone we encounter. Love and community are born into our vision softly like a butterfly.

External events lose their power as we gain composure when surprises enter our lives. We discover a wisdom just waiting to be enjoyed. Relaxation influences our bodies. We feel a well-being associated with living in such a wonderful place. We let go of those external events of the past that incite negativity. We are uplifted and strengthened by feeling a soundness and a wholeness. Isaiah 30:5.

Focus on this moment as we tune in to the energy that is always there. We are free to find new sensual awareness. We feel a oneness with ourselves. Body and mind and soul are synchronized, and harmony flows smoothly. Love is invisible mystery and it's there in infinite layers.

Unexpected joy finds us going deeper and deeper and easily into infinite possibilities. Joyful experiences do have an eternal focus. These may reflect an inner focus on images, imaginings, and reminiscences.

Catch yourself in this mental time travel and refocus your attention on the here and now.

Anticipation of the Second Coming

We believe in a Second Coming of Jesus. The return of Jesus will happen suddenly and unexpectedly. Paul wrote that the Second Coming of Jesus will be like a thief in the night. I Thessalonians 5.

We are told that we should be prepared for only God knows on which day Christ will appear. Jesus told the parable of the wise and foolish virgins to enable his followers to understand the important truth. We are to be prepared.

Jesus tells us that unexpected day or night will be the best time ever if we remain committed and watchful verses being careless in our words and actions and spiritual growth.

Billions of people wait for the Second Coming. Few stay alert to Jesus' return. After the resurrection, Jesus spent 40 days with his disciples before he went up to heaven. As the disciples watched him ascend, two angels encouraged the disciples with this promise that someday Christ would return: "Men of Galilee, why do you stand gazing up into heaven? This same Jesus, who was taken from you into heaven, will so come in like manner as you saw him go into heaven." Acts 1:11.

Jesus said the same thing himself. John 14:1-3. Jesus' coming will not be a secret. It will be an unexpected surprise to those who are unprepared. I Thessalonians 4:16.

God is infinitely holy. We slip into evil, injustice, and sin. God is altogether awesome. Unexpected events occur frequently. Be alert. Be prepared. Expect the unexpected. Isaiah 40:31.

The spiritual journey is thrilling. Jesus' coming will bring us joy. The surest mark for the waiting Christian is not faith or love, but joy.

Chapter Ten

Inciting Joy in the Committed Life

The committed life involves our decisions that make everlasting things happen. Most are committed to their spouse, their children, their vocation. Commitment brings a special joy as life unfolds from getting married, finding a career, or moving to a new place. A.A. Milne encouraged us in writing: "Promise me you'll always remember that you are braver than you believe, and stronger than you seem, and smarter than you think."

Commitment helps us work through obstacles that appear to be impossible. Commitment makes it easier to focus and keep moving forward. Psalm 139:9-12. Commitment transforms a promises into a reality. Commitment makes time when there is none.

The Holy Spirit catalyzes the situations that brings a commitment to action. As our spirits are filled with love and grace, we gain a special insight into how best to show our compassion.

Commitment gives us hope as a word is said and an ember almost goes out. Something happens and joy is ripped from our breast, thrown to the ground, torn, crushed as the committed stand hurt and confused, empty, and joyless. We take compatibility tests. We list the red flags. Each relationship is unique to each person. Commitment is not the same thing as love.

Feeling the need to end something that has brought joy when it passes the casual stage involves the issue of commitment. There is nothing wrong with wanting to enjoy what you have now. The inability and willingness to think about the next stage of a relationship suggests a fear of commitment. Negative feelings make the possibilities for deep joy impossible.

Commitment Keeps the Door to Joy Open

Joy is never gone forever. But we know it is inside us, therefore, God is in control. Those committed to the love and grace of God know security. Paul mentions joy 14 times in his letter to the Philippians. He was in prison when he expressed his commitment. That cell was ugly, dark, and damp. There were no toilet facilities. The meals were far from nourishing.
I Corinthians 4:11-13, II Corinthians 11:24-29. Paul's joy was obviously indestructible.

Enduring indescribable pain, lonely isolation, disappointments he had what he describes as fruit of the spirit. Joy incites love, frees us of anxiety, causes us to realize that God is there. Committed to kindness and tender gentleness, there is no room for gruff and unkind words.

Serving others is a pleasure. Being content in all circumstances, joyful people have calmness under pressure. Joy sets us free, so we never have to play games any longer. Nehemiah 8:10.

Dietrich Bonhoeffer said, "It is remarkable that I am never quite clear about the motives for any of my decisions." Indestructible joy is ours because Christ lives in you. Commitment opens the gates to let joy flow out of use.

Without joy, we are closed up tight, letting pride and inhibition control this mighty river of joy. My smile betrays my commitment. Others instantly smile right back. No matter how brusque ordinary people look, they smile back.

Nailing down the desires that move our acting in the world feels like trying to catch the wind or find our bearing on an endless sea. Psalm 139:9. Even there, the Psalmist wrote, in the swell of our emotions, the Spirit is leading on, holding us safely. Psalm 139:10. We find joy in the ordinary.

Inciting joy in commitment comes from what we are motivated to do, to keep on doing and getting better every day. Commitments uplift our souls. The Holy Spirit leads us, examining our desires. Read Psalm 37:3-11. We move from identifying what we want into attaining what we want. The psalmist shows our first step is to simply trust, do good, live today, and feed on he faithfulness of God. When our hearts are delighted in the reality of our life wholly enmeshed in God. Psalm 37:5-6.

Commitment to a larger purpose than us enlivens and empowers. Being committed brings visualizations of new possibilities. Breakdowns are transformed into breakthroughs so that ordinary people engage in effective action. Commitment draws on resources and capacities you may not know you have. Share your joy each day. Simple interactions build our faith, testimony, and commitment. Be committed to finding new people in your circle of friends. Look for God in the ordinary. Commit to discovering new areas of service.

The Miracles Beyond Impossibility

Intimate relationships grow into miracles. Ordinary people possess the magic to accomplish things in their relationships that appear impossible for the average person.

Each of our life journeys is our own personal experience. Spiritual integration begins out of our compassion and deep love for life. Until God is embodied as fully as possible and life is fully embraced, the life journey has not been completed. This spiritual path prepares the ground for realization that grace will come when the time is right.

Spiritual seekers think that enlightened commitment is a non-stop experience. Actually, it is quite ordinary. Commitment is the bridge to authentic experience of love and gratitude. Humility is a by-product of the spiritual journey. Messiness and imperfections of being a human, even the most unspeakable acts are part of our personal drama. We open our eyes to the deep spirituality of being loved, shortcomings and all, by a God who embraces us in the midst of our unpredictable lives. (Michael Yaconelli, *Messy Spirituality*, pp. 14-17)

This book began with the friendship of Jesus and his disciples. These were ordinary men. After Jesus' crucifixion and resurrection, Luke tells about two people walking from Jerusalem to Emmaus. They talked about the surprise of the empty tomb. They soke of what might have happened. They thought they were talking with an ordinary stranger. This stranger had an extraordinary knowledge regarding the Messiah. The walk and talk had incited joy. As he blessed the bread for supper, they realized that the stranger was Jesus. Jesus mysteriously disappeared.

They did not understand their encounter. They grew up together as friends on a common journey. That is commitment in action. Commitment incites joy and a quality of living to our potential. Commitment breeds motivation. We act persistently and passionately. Commitment is giving our all. It is never a half-hearted effort. Commitment is all or nothing.

Commitment involves sacrifice. We give up some good things to gain something much better. Few people would invest four years of college and four years in seminary if they know the details and unexpected disappointments without a long-term focus. Students do not understand their needed sacrifices.

129

Without honest guidance of ordinary people as to the realities of life after schooling, they will not have any foresight.

Doing What Unsuccessful People Are Unwilling to Do

Successful people do what unsuccessful people are not willing to do. Academic and vocational advisors need to be honest about what ordinary people will endure: small or dead-end appointments or calls, low wages, little respect, and taking responsibility for what is.

We need commitment to discipline to deepen and strengthen us. We must develop special spiritual discipline. Prayer, fasting, and study, solitude, submission, confession, and celebration invoke the presence of God. We live beyond ourselves.

Real change takes place as we make a conscious attempt to adopt the qualities that fit into the will of God. II Peter 1:8-9.

We need to practice spiritual disciplines, so we develop healthful habits that produce character. This in turn brings spiritual growth. The fruit of discipleship comes from years of practice. Love, grace, and joy blend together the disjointed aspects of our journey.

A golden thread of commitment winds it way through life's road involving human relationships. They gain strength and beauty with a commitment to love.

Ordinary people step forward boldly. They go on without any answers or what their commitment will involve. I admire those with courage and honest apprehension. With my own 70 years of sharing the joy of the Lord, I know that the road to success can be long and hard. Commitment is not a sentimental endeavor. Commitment crosses boundaries and puts the committed in constant peril. They face ridicule and even worse endings. Lifetime commitment courts death. John 15:13. If our commitments do not end in our physical death. It means living for the coming kingdom in disciplined fellowship.

The task before us is not easy. We are committed to love people respectfully in our abusive culture. We cannot to this alone. Loving commitment is a gift. Relationships are commitments. What makes befriended another for her own sake such a joy is that the relationship is oriented toward inclusivity. This commitment widens our circle of love. With this wider commitment to befriend God and others with loving solicitude, the world becomes a sad and lonely place.

Friendship with Jesus is the foundation of true friendship for other people. Jesus promised that when two or three are gathered together in my name, there am I in the midst. Matthew 18-20.

When committed friends of Christ come together to share, to laugh, to talk, he is with us. Strangers become open and honest with each other. Being together in commitment teaches us to reappreciate the ordinary things that make life so delightful. This kind of intimacy gives us the relaxation we need by the atmosphere of mutual acceptance. When we live in this way, it is a deeper way to encounter friends and strangers. And when we do, we make the God in our own lives more visible to them. John 15:9.

Each person is able to incorporate spiritual discipline. Our goal is not to follow someone else's spiritual practices. Commitment is grounding us in God so that we have more ability to live the life God wants for us.

Together, we dare to ask if we are in tune with God, or if our willfulness is standing in the way of the Spirit. Those special few relationships we call irreplaceable are our lifelines. They bail us out of stormy seas. They are worth tons of gold.

When friends don't accept each other as they are, they might regress into unhealthy judging, analyzing, or doubting. Friendships are not static. The deepest and best friendships do not remain the same. Real friends are committed to growing and changing alongside their friends. Our commitment involves being flexible, tolerant, patient, and resilient.

Real friends set boundaries. They keep their emotional life up to date. Life is easier the lower we keep our expectations. This becomes a powerful recipe for a more peaceful soul.

Life-long friendships are among life's rarest gems. The joy we feel in another's company and the way we love as committed Christians is truly our destiny. This kind of ordinary gift of spiritual friendship is a dim reflection of the love we are destined to enjoy for eternity.

Commitment to Ultimate Fulfilling Love

Ultimate commitment means ultimate love. Love is the fulfillment of our ultimate quest. Commitment is to love as the skeleton is to the human body. My chiropractor, Dr. Bryan Hufstader, says there is nothing amorous about a skeleton, but where would the body be without its strength and substance?

Real friends challenge us to think in new ways. God uses our commitment to ourselves and others to open our eyes and inciting joy. There are the joyful surprises of the love of God. We are nearest to God when we love.

Pure love exists only in God. Something wonderful happens when we surrender our loves. Love activates commitment through the Holy Spirit. Ordinary love is changed from natural to supernatural love. Uniting God's Spirit with our spirit produces positive joy into our lives. God forms loving nature into us. We can then fully accept ourselves. We become a vessel for letting love flow out to others.

We need others. People are not just an inconvenience. As we awaken to the love of God in our lives, we are more capable of loving others. And we become more enabled to love ourselves.

This is the miracle of grace. The Holy Spirit directed my love and empowered my commitment before I experienced God's kind of love. I savored the taste of divine love before I could demonstrate love to the world. I John 4:7-8. Ordinary people remain as passive instruments, plain old empty vessels containing divine love. A choice to love depends on our level of commitment.

Love is not magic. There is no secret formula for being intimate with a loving God. It comes as we are quietly listening. God embraces ordinary souls tenderly.

God cares less about the words we say, the titles and degrees we earned. We must put energy and our desire for unconditional love. We need an intense commitment.

Being a committed disciple is not a matter of credentials. Love and grace are the foundations of eternal joy. Be confident in what you believe in. Stay aligned to what you believe in. Take joust a moment to look back at how far you've already come.

Listen to your mind and body and soul and reward yourself with time for reflection. We not created to become machines. Take care of yourself and provide the self-love tat is essential to your well-being.

Feel grateful each day. It is so easy to get lost in our life journeys. The trip is a process. Every single moment is a gift.

Bibliography

Ackerman, John. *Listening to God: Spiritual Formation in Congregations*. Bethesda, Maryland: Alban Institute, 2001.

Ahrens, A.H. and Gary Sypeck, "No Longer Just a Pretty Face: Fashion Magazine Depictions of Ideal Female Beauty from 1959-1999," *International Journal of Eating Disorders*, 31, 29-49, 2004.

Bergman. Alan, Marilyn Bergman, and Marvin Hamlisch. "Ordinary Miracle" Lyrics. Nashville: ATV Music Publishing, 2022.

Bonanno, George. "Loss, Trauma, and Human Resilience: Have We Underestimated the Human Capacity to Thrive after Extremely Aversive Events," *American Psychologist*, 59, 20-28.

Bonhoeffer, Dietrich. *Life Together: The Classic Exploration of Christian in Community*. New York: Harper and Sons, 2009.

Brown, Brene. *Atlas of the Heart: Mapping Meaningful Connection and the Language of Human Experience*. New York: Random House, 2021.

Bullard, George W. *Pursuing the Full Kingdom Potential of Your Congregation*. Saint Louis: Chalice Press, 2005.

Bunyan, Paul. *The Pilgrim's Progress from This World to That which Is to Come*. Grand Rapids, Michigan: Christian Classics Ethereal, 1975.

Bunyan, Paul. *The Pilgrim's Progress Study Guide*. Pensacola, Florida: Chapel Library Books, 1980.

Bush, Peter. *Where 20 or 30 Are Gathered*. Herndon, Virginia: Alban Institute, 2006.

Buxbaum, Yitzhak. *Jewish Tales of Mystic Joy*. San Francisco: Jossey-Bass, 2002.

Canfield, Jack, Mark Hansen, and Fabrizio Mancini. *Chicken Soup for the Chiropractic Soul*. Deerfield Beach, Florida: Health Communications, 2003.

Carroll, Lewis. *Alice in Wonderland through the Looking Glass*. New York: T.Y. Crowell and Company, 1893.

Creel, Ann Howard. *The Magic of Ordinary Days*. New York: Penguin Publishing Company, 2011.

Covey, Stephen. *The Seven Habits of Highly Effective People: Powerful Lessons in Personal Change*. New York: Free Press 2004.

Cunningham, Charles. *The Mystery of the Ordinary*. San Francisco: Harper and Row, 1989.

Foster, Richard. *Celebration of Discipline*. San Francisco: Harper and Row, 1978.

Jackson, Phil. Sacred Hoops: *Spiritual Lessons of a Hardwood Warrior*. New York: Hyperion Publishers, 1995.

Killinger, John. *Bread for the Wilderness, Wine for the Journey*. Waco, Texas: Word Books, 1976.

Kondrath, William. *Facing Feelings in Faith Communities*. Herndon, Virginia, Alban Institute, 2008.

Lee, John. *Growing Yourself Back Up: Understanding Emotional Regression*. New York: Three Rivers Press, 2002.

Levison, Jack. Fresh Air: *The Holy Spirit for an Inspired Life*. Brewster, Massachusetts: Paraclete Press, 2012.

Lewis, C.S. *The Four Loves*. New York: Harcourt Brace Jovanovich, 1960.

Lewis, Karoline. *Rereading the Shepherd Discourse Back into the Fourth Gospel,* New York: Peter Lang Publishers, 2008.

Lightbody, Gary and the group Snow Patrol. "Chasing Cars," single on album "Eyes Open," Sidney, Australia: Universal Publishing Group, 2006.

Lucado, Max. *How Happiness Happens: Finding Lasting Joy in a World of Comparison, Disappointment, and Unmet Expectations*. San Francisco: Harper/Collins Publishing, 2022.

Marney, Carlyle. *He Became Like Us*. Nashville: Abingdon Press, 1965.

McReynolds, James. *An Ounce of Prevention*. Saint Louis: Christian Life Commission, 1974.

McReynolds, James. *Children in My Heart*. Bristol, Tennessee: Bristol Business Services, 1959.

McReynolds, James. *Joy Comes in the Mourning: Love Is Forever*. Cleveland, Tennessee: Parson's Porch Books, 2020.

McReynolds, James. *The Spirit of Joy Church*. Cleveland, Tennessee: Parson's Porch Books, 2019.

McReynolds, James. *The Silence of the Church: The Spiritual Struggle with Sexuality*. Cleveland, Tennessee: Parson's Porch Books, 2017.

O'Day, Gail. "I Have Called You Friends," *Baylor University Center for Christian Ethics on Friendship*. Waco Texas: Baylor University Publishing, 2008.

Robert, Dana. *Faithful Friendships: Embracing Diversity in Christian Community*. Grand Rapids, Michigan: William B. Eerdmans Publishing Company, 2020.

Ross, Maggie. *The Fire of Your Ordinary Life*. New York: Paulist Press, 1983.

Stafford, Tim. *Do You Sometimes Feel Like a Nobody?* Grand Rapids, Michigan: Zondervan Publishing House, 1980.

Swartz, James and Joseph Swartz, *Seeing David in the Stone*. Carmel, Indiana: Leadership Books Press, 2007.

Tournier, Paul. *The Adventure of Living*. Trans. Edwin Hudson. New York: Harper and Row, 1965.

Tylka, Thomas L. *Positive Psychology Perspectives on Body Image: A Handbook*. New York, Guilford Press, 2011.

Van Kaam. *The Mystery of Transforming Love*. Denville, New Jersey: Dimension Books, 1994.

Van Kaam. *The Roots of Christian* Joy. Denville, New Jersey: Dimension Books, 1988.

Weatherhead, Leslie. *The Significance of Silence*. New York: Abingdon-Cokesbury, 1955.

Willard, Dallas. *The Spirit of the Disciplines: Understanding How God Changes*. San Francisco: Harper, 1988.

Yaconelli, Michael. *Messy Spirituality*. New York: MFJ Fine Communications, 2007

Notes about the Author

James McReynolds has dedicated his life to helping ordinary people become extraordinary. His commitment to sharing Christ with the world has resulted in millions of souls come to enjoy their life journeys.

In a time when traditional publishing is in turmoil and transition, he is passionate about writing and pursuing his calling.

Whether you received this book as a gift, borrowed it from a friend, or bought it for yourself or a group as you read the words of an ordinary man, who has been called me of the most refreshing voices of our times.

God has an incredible dream for you. We are just passing through in our brief earthly journey. We are pilgrims on a journey toward the eternal city of God.

One aspect of this author's ministry is to observe people and find what is not working. Life is amazing. Good things happen to ordinary people and if we believe it wholeheartedly, we will incite joy. Keep patiently looking for the good in everyone. The more you discover it, the more you will live it. The more that you emulate it, the more you will inspire others to discover truth, beauty, and goodness.

McReynolds has a sense of mission. He communicates concepts of joy that can never be taken away. Uniquely suited for his calling as a communicator, he did not choose his mission. The still voice of God assured him that he has been in right places at the right times.

Staying open to the possibilities brings about a whole new level for life's journey. Speaking and writing are part of his specific mission. During 70 years of serving as an ordained minister, he has devoted his life to teaching ordinary people how to create an atmosphere for joy that has revolutionized the lives of countless people.

Contact the author at 320 North 4th Street, Elmwood Nebraska 68349. His email is joyminister@windstream.net. His phone is 1-402-994-2370.

He is available for speaking to secular and religious groups.

Other Books Published by Parson's Porch Books, 2011-2023
Written by James McReynolds

The Spirituality of Joy: The Least Discussed Human Emotion, 2011

The Joy of Preaching: Encountering Jesus through the Word of God, 2013

Dancing with God: A Theology of Joy, 2016

The Silence of the Church: The Spiritual Struggle with Sexuality, 2017

The Spirit of Joy Church, 2019

Joy Comes in the Mourning: Love Is Forever, 2020

The Joy of Prayer: The Way to Intimacy with God, 2020

The Joy of the Kingdom: Envisioning the Great Commission, 2020

Walking with God in the Garden: Journey in Jouissance, 2021

Joy in the Seasons of Life: Walking Each Other Home to God, 2021

Living the Dream: Amazing Adventure in Marriage, 2021

Joy Beyond the Walls of This World, 2021

The Gospel of Joy: Global Impact of the Ministry of Joy to the World, 2022

Joy Filled Souls: It Is Well with My Soul, 2022

Grace Revealed: Bring Joy to the World, 2022

The Strength of Being Tender, 2022

Peace that Passes All Understanding, 2022

www.ingramcontent.com/pod-product-compliance
Lightning Source LLC
Chambersburg PA
CBHW071006120626
46546CB00003B/958